HOW TO BECOME
A MEDIUM

A STEP-BY-STEP GUIDE TO CONNECTING WITH THE OTHER SIDE BY SPIRITUAL MEDIUM

SECOND EDITION

MARY-ANNE KENNEDY

LIBRARY TALES PUBLISHING

PRINTED IN THE UNITED STATES OF AMERICA

LIBRARY TALES PUBLISHING
www.LibraryTalesPublishing.com
www.Facebook.com/LibraryTalesPublishing

For general information on our other products and services, please contact our Customer Care Department at 1-800-754-5016, or fax 917-463-0892. For technical support, please visit www.LibraryTalesPublishing.com

Library Tales Publishing also publishes its books in a variety of electronic formats. Every content that appears in print is available in electronic books.

978-1-956769-16-6
978-1-956769-17-3

Drawings by Vancouver-based, internationally-
exhibited artist Toni Latour.
www.tonilatour.com

TABLE OF CONTENTS

MARY-ANNE KENNEDY

DEDICATION

For my Dad, whose transition to spirit was a tremendous gift of love and transformation in my life.

For my children and husband, whose love and support allow me to learn, expand, and progress. Your love is a gift that I hold sacred.

For my family, friends, and 'soul sisters', whose encouragement, support, and love nourish me in beautiful ways.

And finally, for spirit. Thank you for trusting me to deliver your healing words - your love - to those left behind.

ACKNOWLEDGMENTS

This book wouldn't be possible without the infinite love and support of my husband, Ryan. We sat together many nights after our children were in bed, with me on one sofa writing, and him on another dozing off. Ryan has been the caring father at home with our two babies after exceptionally busy work days of his own, all so I could partake in the vast number of experiences that have come to shape my own spiritual and personal truths, and ultimately this book.

I meet with many wonderful people each week for private mediumship readings and spiritual guidance. During many of those meetings, my amazing mother, Esther, takes the best care of my children, who love their Nanna so much, and so do I.

My two children, August and Culzean, fill my life with the kind of love that can't be described with mere words. They inspire me everyday with their innate ability to connect with the spirit world. And my daughter especially, who's never afraid to say to anyone who will listen that she sees the spirit lights of our loved ones follow her around - she is so in tune. Because of my beautiful children, my life is rich.

I have immense gratitude for my sisters and brother, and my other family and friends who have supported my life as a Medium. I know it's not always easy to hear about experiences with the dearly departed! But still I was loved and encouraged to share my light. And for that I am grateful.

My life as a Medium wouldn't be possible without those wonderful people, my clients, who have trusted me to channel some of the most important people in their lives. I'm always honored beyond measure to provide a bridge between this world and the next, to prove that souls survive death - that love survives.

Over the years I have learned that so much of what happens on the healing journey is beautifully orchestrated by spirit. Where we think we might meet or find someone like a Medium just by chance or have a seemingly random spiritual experience, spirit knew all along that these things would come to pass. And I thank them for the sweeping number of amazing people, their loved ones here in the physical, that they have sent to sit with me.

Finally, I must thank my spirit guides, angels, and loved ones on the other side who, like lighthouses, have guided me through all of my spiritual journeys. Because of these wonderful journeys guided by spirit, I have come to know my life as incredibly beautiful and full of treasures. Thank you, my guides, angels, and loved ones, for always being available and never leaving my side.

FOREWORD
By Peggy Wewiora

My life journey has been full with family, my husband, my daughter and friends. I have always said that I have no regrets despite bumpy patches and personal loss. No regrets, but no great passion either - nothing special just for me - about me.

Several years ago I started thinking about what's next. Thinking, yes, but not changing anything. I understood that I needed to find my spiritual side but did nothing to figure out what that meant.

Last year I suffered the loss of my husband, and within months, my daughter's husband. In my grief I sought comfort in mediumship to hopefully hear from spirit.

This is what led me to Mary-Anne and opened my eyes and heart to new possibilities. Through meeting Mary-Anne, I now understand what I need to do to fulfill my spiritual being. She not only has connected me with loved ones in spirit with amazing accuracy, but she has also introduced me to methods to heal myself. My physical world has expanded, and I am comforted.

With her guidance and support, I am learning to be open to what is possible. Most importantly she has described and shown me the power of meditation - the foundation of a balanced and spiritual life.

My life journey has added new pathways of comfort and healing.

And I have great gratitude for her guidance and compassion. I know that her teachings will provide the foundation for others to enhance their inner spirit as it has mine.

AUTHOR'S FOREWORD

It seems like a lifetime ago that this book, *How to Become a Medium: A Step-by-Step Guide to Connecting with the Other Side* was first released. At the time, I was working with clients local to me and indeed around the globe, giving private and gallery mediumship readings. I was teaching mediumship to students in group workshops and classes, and, I was a mom and wife raising a young family. And while all these things are still true, so much has changed.

The nature of spirit is the same as it has ever been. It is love. And how we communicate with them is also the same - nothing has changed over the past years. However, as we come out of what is hopefully the tail-end of a global pandemic in 2022, the way we connect spirit to their loved ones here in the physical world has hugely changed. How we communicate with each other, human-to-human, has changed. In 2015 when this book was first released, nine out of ten readings I would deliver would be in-person. Today in 2022, and in fact since March of 2020, one hundred percent of all private readings, all gallery readings, all speaking engagements, have been virtual.

People often ask me, "Does it still work the same? Can you connect with spirit for me, even though we are not sitting in the same room together?". It is fascinating to most that the process is exactly the same, and that as mediums, we do not need to be face-to-face with the folks we are reading for. The truth is, we are not bound by time and space in spirit communication, so physical boundaries or separations are totally irrelevant to the process.

As years have passed and my own life has evolved and widened in so many ways, I find myself easily being able to edit chapters in this book, or add to them. Sharing greater knowledge and instruction deepens with experience, and so it makes sense that seven or eight years later, I would be in a position to want to make the material more robust and more useful. I think most authors releasing a second edition feel similarly. But over the years, an abundance of readers have sent letters, emails, and shared reviews that this book was JUST what they needed to get started in mediumship. No more, and no less. And for this reason, this book remains the same as the original, and the higher-level learning for the more advanced medium can be found in my forthcoming second book. With the same enthusiasm as I held in my heart seven years ago, I look forward to helping you along in your journey with spirit.

INTRODUCTION

"I wish I could do what you do". I have heard it hundreds of times. And my response is always the same: "You can!" Honestly - you can! I'm a Spiritual Medium, and I talk to the dearly departed. When I say that you can do it too, I'm not saying it to pay lip service to any of the wonderful people I meet. I'm saying it because it's been proven to me over and over again that anyone who wants to learn to connect with spirit, can. I have yet to meet an adult who wished to perceive spirit who could not.

I'm not saying it's always an easy process; some find it easy and some find it harder. And just like anything else, some people will be better at being a Medium than others. But all of that aside - if you decide to dedicate whatever time it takes, stick to the process, release expectations of getting to a certain place by a certain time, and put faith in spirit that what unfolds for you is meant to happen, then you will be successful. You will! And if you're reading this book, then I'm going to help you get there.

This book is intended to start you on your journey of mediumship and spirit communication, and it begins with the same first step involved in most spiritual development endeavors: meditation. If you've already begun your inner journey and have learned to meditate, not to worry - this book is still for you! In this step-by-step guide to connecting with the other side, learning to meditate is only the first step of many.

It's important to know that over the next several chapters, the information and guidance I present to you is based on my knowledge and wisdom gained through extensive experiences with spirit. And like most spiritual practitioners or teachers, I've also expanded my knowledge and understanding of spiritual concepts and theories through many vicarious learning experiences with other spiritual teachers, mentors, colleagues, or texts. Through reading this book, you will also be learning in these two distinct ways: vicariously through me as your guide and teacher, but also experientially through the exercises presented. It's through this sequence of learning that real knowledge and wisdom is gained. Vicarious learning leads us to the belief stage, which like all aspects of learning, is an essential step. But it's through the experiential learning, those authentic, genuine, first-hand experiences, that our truths are formed - where belief makes way for knowing - where we no longer say we believe in something, but rather we can say we *know* it's true.

Every Medium is different, and I don't think one way of connecting with spirit is better than another - there are just different ways, and some will work for you and some won't (as is the case with most things). We all have our own personal techniques or approaches that work best for communicating with the spirit world and delivering a powerful reading. So it's important to understand that what I teach in this book is my own process of mediumship that works for me, which will inevitably be different from others. And I encourage you to make amendments or alterations to any of the exercises or suggestions I make to accommodate what works best for you. After all, this is the beginning of *your* journey, and you are the navigator of this vessel!

You've picked up this book to learn to be a conduit between this world and the next. And your motivation might be to speak with your own loved ones on the other side, or it might be to communicate with the loved ones of other people to help bring about healing and understanding here in the physical world. Or you may not have any idea what your motivation is or what you'd like to do with the new skills you're about to learn. And either way, it's okay. You don't have to have your journey all mapped out. In fact, with all things spiritual, it's better to not push the river (that is, don't drive a hard plan), but rather let the river flow all by itself. Throughout the course of this book you'll be embarking on an adventure of discovery, and part of the adventure is to learn what works for you and what doesn't - so allow for experimentation, and have fun!
I don't believe any spiritual teachers here in the physical world can unerringly be called 'experts' in spirituality. Why not? Because I've learned spiritual work, knowledge, and wisdom is infinite. Just when you've grasped a concept about how spirit and energy works on the grand scale, something new is presented to you, and from there, you can extend and expand even farther. And so like many other spiritual teachers, I don't write this book from the position of a self-proclaimed expert on spirituality, because I'm not convinced such a thing exists. I do, however, know that many of us are farther along in our journeys of growth, healing, and expansion, and from these perspectives are able to

offer teaching, guidance, and support to those who aren't quite there yet. My intention and goal for this book is that it becomes a tool of significance in your learning of mediumship.

There are many idioms that are customarily used to represent the place we go to when we die. For the purposes of your understanding in reading this book, I will use the terms heaven, the hereafter, spirit, the spirit world, and the other side interchangeably to describe that place.

My hope is that this book will start you on a path of discovery and experience, allowing you to learn to silence the internal dialogue that so often prevents us from perceiving spirit. More than half of the process of learning any type of spiritual work is learning to be quiet - inside and out. Once we've mastered this skill, we're more easily able to part the veil between our world and vibration (here in the physical) and spirit's in the ethereal. The other half of the process is dedicated to learning how to perceive spirit, how to communicate with them, and then how to deliver their messages in an accurate and loving way to someone here who wants and needs to hear from their dearly departed.

There are some topics in mediumship that I won't delve into here, and they're mostly related to lower energies, hauntings, or spirit rescue work. In my professional practice, these aren't aspects of work that I do (by choice) simply because they aren't in my calling. From the beginning, I've always chosen to work only with spirit that walks exclusively in the light. There are some absolutely excellent practitioners who do amazing work clearing lower energies, and so if this is something you also have no draw to, simply leave it to them! Spiritual practitioners work together all the time

- we can't possibly spread the light all by ourselves! But comfort-boundaries aside, it's my honest belief that when we work in the light and follow its path, it's our birthright to be safe, and our angels and guides in the spirit world help to care for us in that regard. Once you know this, there is no real space for fear or discomfort.

As for skeptics out there, you are welcome to read on! It's not my intention or desire to change anyone's mind about spirit and whether or not a soul exists. I've met and given readings to my share of skeptics or people 'on the fence', and I think it's a healthy thing. After all, I don't just believe new things presented to me. If they ring true - that is, if my higher self or intuition acknowledges the information in an affirming way, then I believe it. But in order to really know something is true, I have to experience it for myself. With respect to skeptics, however, I will say this: Some of the most beautiful transformations through mediumship experiences are born out of those who are the most *unlikely* to be transformed.

Before learning to be a Medium, I had positive experiences with other Mediums that lead me to say to myself, "It must be true, because there's no way they could have known all of that stuff." But still, it never became truth for me until I did it myself - until I had first-hand experience with seeing, feeling, and talking to a being that didn't exist like you and me sitting here. And even then, everything they showed me had to be consistently validated as correct or true by someone who knew them here in the physical world. When that happened, over and over again, my own personal truth was formed: We are spirits or souls first, there is continuation of the existence of our spirits and souls after physical death, and that communication between the physical and spiritual worlds is possible and happens all the time.

It's also my experience and observation that tells me not only does spirit communication happen all the time, but the veil (the distinction or point of separation between the physical world and the spirit world) is ever-thinning - almost on a daily basis. This means more and more people are connecting with and becoming aware of the other side. Have you ever noticed that conversations about Mediums or signs from loved ones who have crossed over are becoming more commonplace? Proof that a spiritual shift, in a positive direction, is taking place on a large scale. How wonderful!

I'm often asked the question, "How did you learn you had this gift?" And here's how I always answer: I wouldn't call what I do a gift. I would sooner call it an ability or skill. For me, the word 'gift' implies that I'm special or unique because of the work I do. But that doesn't ring true for me. As I said, while some people are certainly better Mediums than others, my experience shows that anyone who has a genuine desire to connect with the spirit world can learn to talk to the dead. It doesn't take being 'special' or 'chosen' to do it...unless you consider anyone and everyone as special and chosen, which definitely isn't a bad thing!

But it isn't lost on me for one second that working as Medium, and being able to connect people here with their loved ones in spirit is a very special thing. Mediums are spiritual and emotional healers-of-sorts, because mediumship, for those who experience it, can be incredibly healing. Knowing that our loved ones aren't dead and gone - knowing that they still exist and are alive and well in the spirit world, is incredibly comforting and gives us tremendous peace.

Another question I'm often asked is whether or not I was born a Medium. Well, the long and short of it is that I don't know. I have no first-hand knowledge of anyone in my ancestry being mediumistic, or having other spiritual abilities. Does that mean there was no one in my family before me who was a Medium? Perhaps. But perhaps not. I'll never know for certain with verifiable proof either way, so to me, it really doesn't matter. I want you to know right now that being born a Medium is not a prerequisite to being a successful one. So if you've ever thought to yourself, "I wasn't born into a family of Mediums, and no one in my lineage was clairvoyant, so I can't do mediumship", just forget about it - it's not true...trust me!

I subscribe to the idea that we plan the major lessons in our life that we need to learn on a soul level, and I also know we have themes or attributes that make up what we do or give to the world in this lifetime. And while everyday is a new learning experience and life is constantly unfolding, I'm comfortable and happy knowing that part of my contribution to the people in my life (friends, family, clients, and you) is to bridge the connection between the spirit world and us here in the physical.

CHAPTER 1
Life and Death at the Same Time

Rather than start at the beginning of my physical life, I will start at the beginning of my spiritual life. But I'll tell you a little bit about my younger years as it relates to spirituality.

I was raised as a Roman Catholic by my wonderful and loving parents. They were dedicated to teaching us (me and my three siblings) to be kind and hard-working people. And I think it's a tremendous acknowledgment of their success as parents that all of their children are in-fact kind, hard-working, and successful in a multitude of ways. Hats off to my Mom and Dad!

I can still remember, clear as day, when my Mom had a Psychic Party at our house. I was eleven years old and was inexplicably drawn to this event (none of my other siblings were very intrigued). I know now that it's no coincidence my Mom had the psychic reader visit our house, but rather synchronicity at its finest! It was the beginning of my spiritual life unfolding.

Just a few weeks before the party, I was watching a talk show about some teens whose parents were practicing pagans (Wiccans, specifically). During the show, the guests did a great job of dispelling myths about witches and dark energy work, and they were sure to highlight the most wonderful and beautiful qualities of the Wiccan way of life. So on the day of the Psychic Party at my house, I gathered up the nerve to ask the psychic reader if she knew anything about Wicca. And wouldn't you know it, she did. Well, sort of. She had a friend who was a solitary practitioner of Wicca, and with my Mom's blessing, she gave me the name and phone number of her friend.

Shortly thereafter, we met and I gained a teacher and mentor in earth-based religion. Amazingly, we are still connected as friends today! I kept my learning a secret from my Dad, but my Mom, my ever-supporting rock, could see that I was being called to this study, and she allowed to me to explore and expand. How lucky are we, when as young people, our parents allow us to nourish what our souls are asking for? I for one, am truly grateful for that.

I began to have a meditation practice, and studied intensely anything that I could get my hands on related to the occult, magic, runes, herbs, spirit, ghosts, and the list goes on. I remember encountering spirit twice as a child, although the way I perceived them is a lot different from how I perceive spirit today. Back then, I saw them the same way I see you - in a very dense, physical form. Today, I see spirit either in my mind's eye, or I see the lights (energy) of spirit with my physical, waking eyes.

My first encounter with spirit as a young person was at a friend's home where I used to spend a lot of time. My friend's mom used to see a psychic too, and the psychic told her there were spirits in her house. One day when I was eleven or twelve, my friend and I were talking about spirits and looking at some of my ghost books in her parents bedroom when we both turned to see a young boy wearing an old 'newsies' hat in the closet. We stayed staring at him, saying to one another, "can you see that?", and he just stared back. After a few minutes of exchanging gazes, we left the room screaming! To this day, I have no idea who that boy was or why he was there.

My second encounter with spirit was following my maternal grandparents' passing. They died very close together, and not long after, they both sat on the end of my bed - I felt the bed go down, and all! It was amazing because while I couldn't actually see them, I knew intuitively it was them, and I wasn't afraid.

You might be asking why the way I perceive spirit changed from when I was a younger person to now. Well, besides the fact that our spiritual abilities change and evolve all the time, I made a distinct decision when setting my boundaries with spirit as an adult (which I'll touch on a little later) that I don't want to see them in a physical way. It's just a preference, and spirit has respected my boundaries so far...with the minor exception of a spirit dog I once saw walk, clear as day, across a small parking lot. But it was okay - he was cute, and I didn't mind!

My pagan practice continued for over fifteen years, and it was wonderful. Through my teenage years and early twenties, I went through the usual young person ordeals and attitudes, and on many occasions didn't practice regularly, if at all. But I would usually find the way back to my altar, and center myself once more.

Then, one cold and sunny February morning when I was twenty-eight and my daughter was six months old, my Dad died. And right then and there, all of my practice and all of my beliefs ended.

Along with my siblings and mother, I sat with my

Dad as he took his last breaths. Truly a moment that, in a haunting way, can never fade from memory. But it was also a tremendous honor to be in the presence of someone who was dying so that they were not physically alone. I am honestly joyful I was able give love and support to my Dad right to the very end of his physical life.

After my Dad's passing, I would openly challenge the spirit world to prove itself to me. I was angry - angry my Dad was gone. I would watch reality television shows that searched for proof of ghosts or spirits just to see if I could be convinced. And I never was. You see, I had always believed that we continue to live on after death, but after losing my dad, I didn't want to believe anymore. Belief wasn't enough. Without knowing for sure, an afterlife just wasn't real to me anymore. I loved my Dad so much and longed so badly to feel him or know he was there, and part of my grief was to not accept anything less than irrefutable proof that he still existed. In grief, some people are okay with believing. But I wasn't. I had to know, one way or another.

If you can, imagine in one moment the joy of having your first born child, looking into their eyes and seeing health, innocence, beauty. And in the very next moment, you're watching your father drenched in anxiety and fear of dying. You see, my Dad had lung cancer and emphysema, and he literally struggled to breath everyday. In the last six months of his life here in the physical world, not a day went by where he didn't panic at the thought that he was dying. Witnessing my Dad's struggle bore in me a level of anxiety and fear I never imagined. But it wasn't until after he died that I realized what a terrible place I was in - emotionally, psychologically, and spiritually.

Following my Dad's transition to spirit, I suffered quite seriously from fear of illness and fear of death. The interesting part was that my fear of illness and death had very little to do with what would happen to me, but everything to do with imagining what would happen to my daughter if I passed away. She was at an age where no one could explain to her what happened to me or why I didn't come home. I would lay awake at night tormented with imagining what would go through her little mind if she had to wonder what happened to Mummy.

Every little ache in my body had me on high alert that something serious was wrong. What's more interesting is that I've met so many mothers over the years who began suffering from the same fears shortly after having children. I feel so lucky to have healed my way through it, because I know how very difficult it is to get to where I am now.

Looking back, I recognize that I made it a point to surround myself with people who acknowledged my anxiety to the point that they would support it - enable it. And even though those people gave that support to me out of love, it really wasn't good for anyone. Most of the conversations around my kitchen, which was a bit of a family hub, were about worries, bad things happening in people's lives, and nurturing fear. This went on for some time, and very slowly, my emotional and spiritual states began affecting my physical body.

One morning not long after my Dad's transition, I woke up and all of the muscles throughout my body were randomly twitching. You can imagine given my state of being, how terrifying this was for me. After doctors and specialists and all the testing that could be done, nothing was abnormal. All the doctors told me the cause was likely rooted in stress. I remember thinking that I had managed to avoid having a physical manifestation of the stress and anxiety in my life up until that point. But now it had finally caught up to me, and I was actually surprised it had taken so long.

Rock-bottom for me happened when my husband,

Ryan, was out having a 'guys night', which he so very much deserved. I was at home with my daughter and my little dog, Jackson, and had just gotten off the telephone with a friend. We had a conversation about our anxieties and fears, which very successfully fed one another's negative states of mind. Similar to 'misery loves company', so too does anxiety. Within minutes of getting off the phone, I found myself overcome with nausea, I was trembling, had numb hands, a rapid heart rate, and I was panicked.

A milder version of this had happened to me once before, so I suspected it was something like an anxiety attack. I called my sister, who was always beyond supportive during my periods of anxiety. And thank the heavens for her, because she talked me through a very scary fifteen minutes, which by the way, was happening in front of my toddler. I did my best to distract her with television and a snack, and to this day, I'm certain she had no idea what was happening to me. But for all the craziness happening in my family room that night, this occurrence became the pivotal moment in my life that spurred me to change.

I had to do something. The very thought that something similar could happen again in front of my daughter was frightening. A friend of mine (ironically the same friend I was having the phone conversation with that triggered my anxiety attack) suggested an acupuncturist in the area who had subsequently worked miracles for her anxiety. So I booked an appointment, and literally, just like that, my life began to change.

CHAPTER 2
The Beginnings of a Journey

I walked out of my first acupuncture treatment acutely aware that I no longer had the fear thoughts I was used to having. My acupuncturist also introduced me to Traditional Chinese Medicine (TCM), which I started taking that very first day.

I made appointments with the acupuncturist twice a week for some time, and then I tapered to once a week, then once a month, and then every so often when I felt like I needed an energetic tune-up, so to speak. I wish I could tell you it was that easy - go see someone, they do all the work for you, and you're all better. But I can't do that with an honest heart.

Very shortly after beginning acupuncture treatment for significant anxiety and fear, I also began attending meditation and psychic development classes. How I stumbled upon these classes was also perfect synchronicity - I don't believe in coincidences.

I was volunteering as a proof-reader for a community magazine and came across an ad in the black and white version of the magazine I was editing. It said, "Meditation and Psychic Development Classes - Register for the Winter Session". At the exact moment I read it, a light flickered in me - something shifted. I knew about the benefits of meditation for people with anxiety or stress, so I checked out the website and registered. It was perfection at its finest for me to be at my worst, and like a beacon, have seen the path illuminated for me. Believe me - it was no easy feat for me to convince myself to go out of the house, even one night a week, to be with a group of strangers who may or may not be welcoming or friendly. But that flicker of light...it pushed me out of my comfort zone and on to the path I was meant to start that day. Looking back, I had never been someone to ignore that gut feeling, or intuition, and I still don't. Try to never ignore it - it serves us well.

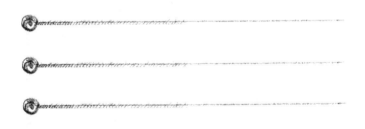

Before starting classes at a local spiritual school, I sat to have my very first mediumship reading at the same place. I sat with an incredibly talented, world-class Medium. I remember the first thing he said when I sat down - he said, "I can see someone sitting in a corner, in 'their' chair, holding a cup of tea and relaxing. Can you understand this?" I was instantly captivated, and I knew in that first moment that my Dad was present. My Dad always sat in 'his' chair with his legs up, usually drinking tea my Mom would make him. What a perfect recognizable way to show himself! I was excited to see what else he was going to say.

After sitting with him for over two hours, the Medium brought through exceptionally accurate proof that he was communicating with my Dad. Some of the things he talked about were special dates, names, things my Dad had seen happen in my life since his passing, and he really brought my Dad's personality and nature to life. I was compelled. And the experience animated me in such a way that I couldn't remain the same person as the day before the reading. I knew something different now - I knew that our souls continue on past physical death. I didn't just believe it - I knew it now. From a purely statistical perspective, the level of his accuracy could not be achieved by coincidence or guessing. The Medium also never opened his eyes during the reading - not once. He never knew what my emotional responses were to the information he was delivering. He just kept going, and it was amazing. Little did I know that day that this person would become my own mentor in the early days of my mediumship development. How lucky I was!

Shortly after my reading, I started classes. So off I went, leaving my toddler at home with her Dad every Wednesday night, and slowly but surely, I started gaining momentum in the way of positive change. Re-learning to meditate changed my life. You see, meditation allows us to disconnect from our physical-selves, and view our life or scenarios in it from an objective or observers perspective. It's as if we're standing outside of ourselves, removed from the emotion of experience, and we're able to recognize truth - and not to mention the state of absolute bliss we experience in meditation. One of the ultimate goals of meditation is to learn to access that state of bliss every day and in every waking moment of life, and not just while in formal meditation. And while I can have an argument with someone or get upset or frustrated just like anyone else, I'm also able to access that state of bliss more easily because I know how to get there and what it feels like. It's like following a short trail of breadcrumbs back to a place that's so familiar. Meditation allows us to clear ourselves out and make room for spirit.

It was in the meditation and psychic development classes that I also learned how I perceive spirit. I learned this by having extensive experiences where spirit would convey information to me during guided meditation. An example of an information exchange with spirit during a guided meditation might happen like this: Journey from your chair, through the top of the roof, passing the treetops into the sky, and finally ending up on a platform in outer space where you can see earth spinning slowly. From there, pass through a doorway, and walk along a golden path to a garden bench. There, sit and ask for a loved one to meet you. Be patient. When they arrive, the way in which you know they're present will be telling of how you perceive spirit. If you see them, you might be clairvoyant (clear-seeing). If you can feel their energy, you might be clairsentient (clear-feeling), or if you simply have an inner knowing they're with you, you might be claircognizant (clear-knowing). During meditation, the natural barriers that exist during waking moments are diminished, and our connection with spirit is made possible and limitless. It's incredible how meditation, alone, can transform a life.

Parallel to my acupuncture treatment and meditation practice, I was also working with a psychotherapist, who also happened to be a practicing Buddhist - lucky me! He offered me some of the most insightful conversations that still resonate with me today. One of the most memorable was when he told me something like, "Your daughter has her own karma. Your life is your life, and she has her own. What happens in her life happens all the same whether you worry about it or not. You can't change any of the things you're scared of, and her journey through life is going to happen however it's supposed to happen." It helped me to recognize that just like me, my daughter has her own path that she's meant to walk. And it was only an illusion that I could control it in some way by trying to keep her safe or keep myself safe for her. Truthfully it took many months for me to accept this, but as I expanded and evolved on a spiritual level, I came to know, accept, and live this truth.

After months of acupuncture, TCM, meditation, psychotherapy, and other spiritual experiences like Past Life Regression, Mediumship Readings, Energy Healings, and the like, I felt like a completely different person. I felt that even to a cellular level, I was different. I vibrated differently, and people noticed it. I felt better than ever before, and I was aligning with the universe. The energy shift was palpable and amazing. Even today, the part of me that existed during those difficult times feels like a faint memory - I can barely connect with who I was then. Truly, once a spiritual shift or awakening occurs, there's no going back. And that's a wonderful thing!

I noticed changes along the way, but it wasn't until over a year later that I stopped and took stock of where and who I was now. It was kind of like waiting for water to cool. The water doesn't go from boiling hot one minute to completely cold the next. As it cools, the temperature gradient slowly drops. It's a slow process (especially if you are watching and waiting for it), but it eventually comes to a desirable temperature.

On the last day of my meditation and psychic development class, our class mentor asked us to not open our eyes at the end of the meditation. She instead asked us to invite a loved one of someone in the room to come close to us. Seems a little far fetched for people who have never communicated with spirit before, right? Wrong! We had learned and made so many connections (with guides, totems, higher selves, and our own loved ones on the other side) over the weeks that most of us were ready to work with other people's spirit loved ones.

I'll always remember the first spirit loved one I ever saw. I had been in the meditation and psychic development class for about twelve weeks, and through validation, the student next to me confirmed the spirit person I saw was indeed her ex-husband. I remember he talked about motorcycles, and even told me his name was Joe, which was correct! I wish it were always that easy to get spirit names - they must have been throwing me a bone - spirit's way of saying "you can do this, keep going". How wonderful! This first experience was the beginning of the unfoldment of my mediumship, and my beautiful and amazing relationship with spirit.

When the next class term rolled around, I decided to enrol in Mediumship Development rather than another round of meditation. I learned through some level of instruction and navigating through the weekly experiences I was having, but I also learned a lot from other Mediums in the classes - some of who were starting out just like me, and some who were experienced.

In these classes I learned a basic framework for communicating with spirit (more on what that is later), how to connect deeper with spirit, and how to build a dictionary of signs and symbols. I also learned that my first and strongest way of communicating with the other side was through sight (clairvoyance). How did I learn this? Well, I more clearly and easily understood what spirit would show me (as pictures or movies in my mind's eye) as compared to information they would communicate in other ways such as having me feel something (as an emotion or internal knowing). My clairvoyant abilities are followed closely in proficiency by clairsentience and claircognizance, and finally by clairaudience (which for me is hearing an internal thought, not a disembodied voice). I also hear sounds from the spirit world - like a whistle, or a cough, or a laugh. When I hear these things and other people around me can't hear them, I know they're coming from the spirit world.

Now, these classes were a little different than what you might see with traditional mediumship. We would sit in a group with anywhere from five to ten Mediums, and we would all take our turns giving a reading in front of everyone, to one or two sitters (people receiving the readings). In many ways it's a hurdle in learning mediumship to give a reading in front of so many people when you're first starting out. Your confidence is low, your dictionary isn't big, and you're inexperienced working with grieving loved ones here in the physical world. You're standing in front of everyone, trying your best to give some healing from spirit. But you know what, the learning opportunity is so magnificent - what better way to learn and improve than to watch experienced Mediums deliver their messages, learn what signs and symbols they use, and allow yourself to be guided and helped by those who are farther along than you? I wouldn't change a thing about those early days of mediumship.

If you ever find yourself on a journey similar to mine, I can't overstate the importance of community and support. The friends I gained in my circle of spiritual practice played a major role in my healing, development, and expansion. People of like-minds can be hard to come by in spiritual work, so take the advice from me - branch out, get out there, and meet people. Don't go it alone! Life is richer with good people in it.

So there I was - I had completed one round of meditation and psychic development classes, and one round of mediumship development classes. It had been two years since my Dad's transition to spirit, and I had moved through the process of grieving. I also transformed my entire being, and now I was working with people who were, in many cases, in the same place I was not that long ago. I was still a student for a long time (we are always students, I know that), and I continued to enroll in several rounds of mediumship development classes to enhance my skills and build my confidence. But once I reached the point that after every reading, less and less direction, guidance, or feedback was needed, I decided to step out on my own.

I should mention that all the while I was taking mediumship development classes, I also offered free readings to anyone who was interested - friends, family, strangers - anyone who would let me practice on them. And my advice for you is to do the same. I even spent a whole summer one year giving readings to a long list of people a friend of mine, Kay, put together for me. Practice, practice, practice - I can't emphasize enough the importance of it in becoming a good Medium!

Some of my mentors said they thought my abilities to connect with the spirit world developed quickly. Perhaps they were right, but we all develop and unfold at the perfect pace, and in perfect timing. I remember seeing friends along the way who took much longer than I did to connect with the other side. But I can tell you this for certain - pace of learning aside, everyone who wanted to learn to channel spirit did learn to do it.

If you find your spiritual development is slower than you'd like, just remember the universe will unravel your path in the timing that's perfect for you. So learn and practice all you can, and I promise spirit will offer you wonderful experiences - really elated moments - along the way to keep you going. Be sure to look out for the jewels - the gems of information that spirit will lighten your heart with in an attempt to say "keep going, and don't give up". For example, if your last couple of practice readings weren't great, and your confidence is waning, ask for spirit to lift *your* spirits by telling you something very specific like their name, or the exact date they were born, or their age at passing. When it happens (and it will happen), be sure to say thank you!

CHAPTER 3
Some Big Ticket Questions

There are some fairly common questions that I'm asked often as a Medium. And since most people who are beginning a spiritual journey will have these questions too, we'll start our learning from this book with addressing them.

The answers I give to these questions come from my understanding from spirit and what they've taught me over the course of my life as a Medium and spiritual practitioner, and the answers are also the sum of all of my own personal experiences with the other side. Some of my answers might be at odds with your beliefs or what you know to be true. But just know that truth is personal and subjective. What's been proven to me over and over again has formed my truth, but you may have had different experiences, so your current truth may be different from mine. However, I subscribe to the idea that truth as we understand it can evolve, and I encourage you to subscribe to a similar idea. I make a point to maintain an openness about what may be, what may not be, or what is at least possible, and you might consider doing the same. Truth is often layered and not simple - though we'd sometimes like it to be. So even when spirit has shown the same explanation for some of these questions over and over again, it's important to acknowledge that we don't have complete awareness of all that is, and therefore may not comprehend the full extent of these most common existential or spiritual questions.

What Happens When We Die?

Spirit tells me that when we pass away and transition to the other side, we're greeted by our loved ones who are already there. We're also greeted by our main spirit guide and our guardian angel. Spirit guides are part of our 'team' of helpers on the other side. Guides are beings who have walked the earth before, but are much farther along in spiritual evolution than we are. At the moment of our birth, we are assigned by source (also known or thought of as god, goddess, universe, etc.) many guides to accompany us on our journey through this lifetime, and one of those guides is usually our 'point person' or main point of contact in the spirit world. Guardian angels are different from spirit guides. Angels are a different kind of being. What I know from spirit and my own guardian angel is that angels never walked here on earth. They vibrate at a much higher or faster rate than spirit loved ones and even our spirit guides. Their purpose is to help and protect us on many levels, and they never leave us. Ever.

Of all the times spirit has shown me their passing, they've never once said it included any pain, any worry, or any fear. They have always shown me they were at peace, blissful, and they *wanted* to go to the hereafter - to the light.

Spirit often talks about things that were happening around them while they were unaware or unconscious before their passing. They also talk about what was happening around them immediately following their passing, proving they are a spirit or a soul outside of their physical body, and that consciousness survives physical death.

I recall before my Dad's transition to spirit while he was still partially lucid, he expressed that he could see his mother - my grandmother - who had passed many years earlier. I felt comforted hearing that, because it proved to me that he wasn't alone at that moment when he had a 'foot' still here in the physical world, and the other in the spirit world.

Spirit has communicated to me many times what it's like on the other side. They perceive and experience things in a different way than you or me. They don't see with eyes, feel with a body, or smell with a nose. But they feel emotion and energy. They are made of light (energy), which includes love. Spirit has shown me (through my third eye, or psychic sight) some of the most beautiful, incredible, and out-of-this-world landscapes that exist in the spirit world. These may not be actual places that tangibly exist like the Grand Canyon or another popular landscape, but they are perceived by spirit beings. So to them (and to us when we're in the spirit world), these places are experienced, felt, and seen, and so they do exist in the spirit dimension.

Through some exceptional experiences with past life regression and life between lives regression, I've also experienced soul memories of what it's like in heaven. And when I had these first-hand experiences with soul memory, it was incredibly validating, because it proved to me that spirit's communication of what the other side is like was accurate. What's more exciting is these beautiful places that exist on the other side may also be accessed by us here in the physical world through deep meditation (or past life/life between lives regression).

You should also know that I don't subscribe to the idea that the hereafter exists in an exact physical location somewhere far away from us. I believe it's here, all around us, on a different level of existence or frequency. At least this is what spirit tells me.

When I Dream About My Loved One, is it a Visitation?

What I know from spirit is most of the time the answer to this question is yes. When we have dreams with more than just a brief cameo by a loved one, it's in fact a visitation from them. During our sleep, we are open in the sense that we aren't inundated with thought, internal analysis, or distractions. So energetically speaking, it's much easier for spirit to enter into our awareness.

A dream visitation is a common way for spirit to communicate with us. These dreams will usually contain a profound experience, or something profound being said or communicated in another way. And you're likely to wake up from the dream feeling different - feeling as though you just had a real, legitimate interaction with someone.

People will often say their loved ones tend to show up in dreams in waves - meaning, not consistently. What I know from spirit is they are more present in our lives during periods where we might need them more for support or guidance, and it's usually these periods when they will make more appearances to us through dreams.

If I Don't Learn to be a Medium for Other People, How Can I Open the Doors to Receive Signs from My Loved Ones on the Other Side?

There are a couple of answers to this question, so here's Part 1 (the easiest way). Learn the signs and symbols that spirit uses often to connect with us here in the physical world (more on what these are later). I can't tell you how many people miss the signs simply because they don't know what they're looking for.

Part 2 - learn to meditate for a deeper connection than just being aware of signs and symbols. Meditation silences our inner dialogue and makes room for us to feel, perceive, and recognize spirit. Sometimes perceiving spirit takes a lot of hard work, but if it's something you want to learn, it *can* be done.

Do Our Loved Ones Know How Much We Miss Them, and Can They See What's Going on in Our Lives Now?

Spirit's answer to this question is this: Always and without exception. They are so deeply connected with us. Our emotions, thoughts, feelings - spirit is aware of them all. In many ways our loved ones on the other side are more in tune with us now than they were here in the physical world. They know us more intimately now than they did before. They can hear and feel our thoughts, our feelings - there is no barrier between us and them.

Spirit is always aware of things going on in our lives since their passing. During mediumship readings, they will often talk about things they've seen you do recently or since their passing to prove they still exist and are part of your life - even from heaven.

What Happens to Our Pets When They Die?

Pets come through during readings with me all the time. Dogs, cats, horses, even hamsters, believe it or not! Based on all of my experiences with seeing and connecting with animals in spirit, I know they go to the same place we do. They even maintain relationships with us when we arrive on the other side. Rarely have I ever seen a pet step forward on their own - they are almost always accompanied by a human loved one on the other side. Love is love - no matter which species are sharing it.

Does Spirit Ever Say Bad Things that We Don't Want to Know?

Spirit doesn't come forward to say 'bad' things. That's not their nature. If something comes up that they're allowed to give you a warning against, or guidance for something to avoid, then they will. But remember, spirit isn't allowed to tell us everything. For example, if we ask them to tell us when we will die, they will very likely not be able to tell us about this part of our divine plan. Think about it - what would you do with that information? You'd be living a stressed out, anxious existence until that day came, and spirit wouldn't want that. Spirit will never come through just to tell you something bad. If they delve into something less than positive, it will always be accompanied by other information so as to empower you with insight and guidance.

When I work with spirit, we (spirit and I) are working for the highest and best for all involved, so it makes sense that they would never intentionally leave you worried or fearful about something. If you leave a spiritual experience feeling uneasy or scared, I would question the accuracy or interpretation of the messenger or Medium more so than the message, itself. In another context, if you find yourself *giving* a message that leaves the recipient feeling that way, I would question the quality of either your connection with the spirit world or your aptitude as a Medium.

What's the Difference Between a Spirit and a Soul?

The answer to this question will help in your understanding of many things we'll discuss in this book, so pay close attention!

There are many analogies that can be used to demonstrate the difference between a spirit and a soul, but I'm going to use the one that was easiest for me to understand when I first asked this question to one of my wonderful spiritual mentors, Lynn.

The soul can be defined as our whole or higher self - the complete spiritual aspect of ourselves that is eternal. It experiences many lifetimes in its progressive journey toward spiritual perfection (meaning having experienced and learned all that is available to be experienced or learned), until it becomes so highly evolved, so enlightened, that lifetimes back on earth are no longer needed. So how does this compare to a spirit?

If we can imagine for a moment that my soul is represented as an orange - a whole orange, made up of many slices. Then imagine the orange slices are the many aspects, or incarnations of my soul, called spirits. So my soul, the whole orange, resides in the spirit world (and is also ever-connected and one with my spirit here on earth). But the slice of the orange, the spirit, that's here experiencing this incarnation, is Mary-Anne. So my unique self, Mary-Anne, is one of many parts (orange slices) that make up my whole self (my soul, or the whole orange). Other incarnations, or lifetimes, that my soul has would be experienced by orange slices other than the slice that I am as Mary-Anne. It's me, Mary-Anne, and the other incarnations, spirits, or orange slices, that make up my soul.

Will My Loved One Still Be on the Other Side by the Time I Get There, or Will They Reincarnate Before I Arrive?

A great question! I will illustrate the answer with an example. Let's say we are asking the question about your grandmother, named Rose. What I know from spirit is that while other aspects of Rose's soul (other orange slices) may make the return to earth for another round before you make it to the other side, the spirit (or orange slice) that was your loved one (your grandma Rose) will always be waiting for you, and a blissful reunion in the hereafter.

As I understand it from spirit, our unique spirits return as one with our soul when this incarnation is over, and each subsequent incarnation to earth is experienced by a new spirit, or different aspect (a different orange slice) of our own soul.

What is a Soul Group?

Have you ever met someone and felt you've known them before, or felt so at ease and comfortable with someone you only just met? Or perhaps there's someone in your life who you are very close with and you can seemingly finish each other's sentences, or read each other's minds or thoughts without speaking a word? If you can answer yes to any of these questions, then the odds are that you have shared many lifetimes with this person, and they are part of your soul group! Did a lightbulb of realization just go off?

So what's a soul group? Well, a soul group is as it's name eludes - a group of souls or beings who we incarnate with, over and over again in different dynamics and relationships, to help us learn our life lessons. As an example, I learned through one past life experience

46

that my mother in this lifetime was my child in a previous lifetime.

While we're on the other side and making our pre-birth plans, we also make arrangements and have agreements with members of our soul group. Our agreements, or contracts, include when and how we'll meet here on earth, and what roles we'll play in each other's lives. For example, my daughter and I agreed that we would meet during this incarnation when I gave birth to her - that would be the moment of our earthly reunion.

CHAPTER 4
Working With Spirit

We all have our own unique journey in life, and along that journey, we inevitably live through experiences and ordeals that cause us to need healing – emotionally, spiritually, and physically. For those who have experienced it, the loss of a close loved one can be devastating – entirely life-changing, and can cause the deepest longing and sadness.

Healing is a process. For some, part of that process includes the desire to communicate with their loved ones, and witness proof of life beyond physical death. It's during mediumship that this opportunity is created. Knowing of the continuation of life, and that our loved ones are okay, can bring tremendous comfort and relief.

Mediumship is the process of communicating with loved ones who have crossed over to the other side. As a Medium, the key goal of your work is to be a clear channel to receive and deliver validation and loving messages from the spirit world. For me at least, it's not an attempt to convince anyone of an afterlife - those who receive validation and messages from spirit can take that information and make their own conclusions about whether or not the hereafter exists.

I practice Evidential Mediumship, which means I bring forward unique information about the spirit I'm communicating with to prove that it's in fact them I'm bringing through. For example, I'm likely to talk about their physical appearance, how they passed, what they did in life, and any other unique and specific information about them. By comparison, one can practice mediumship (communicating with the spirit world) without bringing through evidence, or proof, that it's a unique loved one coming through. An example of mediumship without evidence would be a Medium saying something like, "I feel a mother energy for you in spirit, and she wants to tell you she loves you very much and is with you often." You may have a mother energy (mother, mother-in-law, grandmother) in spirit, and she may be telling the Medium how much she loves you, but in the absence of providing specific information about your unique mother energy, nothing has been proven.

Now, I'm not saying that evidential mediumship is better than non-evidential mediumship, it's just my preference, and that's for one reason, alone: My purpose for channeling loved ones in spirit is about bringing through the messages they want to give, but it's also more importantly, from my perspective, about demonstrating the existence of a soul - that it survives death, and that we all continue to exist in the most beautiful place imaginable. And I believe the combination of validation and messages serves as proof of the continuation of life after physical death, and demonstrates that we are never alone - that our connection of love still exists.

Before we set out on the practice part of this chapter, I want to preface it with this: Just like anything else you want to be proficient in, don't do all of your learning in one place or from one resource. Experience different perspectives, learn though different avenues, research many published works, and create a dialogue with others from whom you can learn. This book alone will get you started, enhance your learning, help you set out and follow a critical path towards developing in mediumship, and it will teach you about many aspects of being a Medium. But I didn't learn to be a good Medium by reading one book, so I encourage you to broaden your learning through many experience and many resources.

This book can and will help you to expand your psychic awareness and teach you to communicate with spirit. But if you've never meditated or learned to silence your internal self, then you have some upfront leg-work to do. Trust me when I tell you that *no one* can teach you to be a Medium without learning to meditate first. But not to worry! I can help you get that leg work squared away.

Part 1: Quieting the Mind

Communicating with spirit isn't as simple as having a conversation with your neighbor. It doesn't take place like a dialogue between two people even though it's presented that way sometimes (although when I'm connecting with my own spirit loved ones, it *is* very much like having a conversation with words - perhaps because I know what their voices sounded like when they were here). I can assure you that it takes knowledge and skill to do it well. Early on in learning mediumship, you will no-doubt connect with spirit - perhaps you'll see them like I do, or maybe you'll feel their energy, or sense them in a different way. And even though it's a tremendous first step to be able to perceive spirit at all, it's really just the beginning. But for now, let's focus on how to achieve this first step.

How can we become aware of energy around us that we can't detect with our usual five senses? Allow me to tell you. First, we have to master or at the very least become adept at silencing our own internal chatter. This takes time and practice (mostly learned through meditation - guided or unguided). I can't overstate the importance of this step. There is no rushing allowed. I promise, if you rush this part, or put an expectation on yourself to master the skill within a defined period of time, you'll be disappointed and frustrated. Tip: Trust in the process that's taking place, trust that you are destined for where you're going, and trust that you'll get there when you're meant to.

Our minds are inundated with clutter. We're usually in a constant pattern of internal dialogue that includes sub-conscious and conscious thoughts about what we're doing, what's happening around us, how we feel about things - the list is literally never-ending! Now imagine this: If spirit is trying to communicate with you in the form of sending you a thought (of theirs), how will you ever recognize that the thought came from them? If your mind is maxed out with your own thoughts all the time, you simply won't be able to recognize spirit's. When we silence our minds and hearts through meditation, room is made for spirit - we open a space of quiet and allow them to enter there.

Learning to meditate isn't an easy task to do without help from a mentor, a good guided meditation audio track, or a book just like this one. Guided meditation CDs or audio tracks are a fabulous way to learn to meditate. There are so many good ones out there - especially those that combine meditation with encountering some form of spirit, such as a guide, angel, or loved one.

Going back to my suggestion about 'not going it alone', one of the best ways to learn to meditate is to find a local class to enroll in. Or you could even try an online meditation group - there are probably more out there than you might expect. I've said it before, and I'll say it again: The value of community in spiritual work is tremendous! Even an online group of like-minded individuals is certain to yield valuable learning experiences, advice, and perspective that you otherwise wouldn't have. But if joining a meditation group just isn't an option for you, guided meditation audio works quite well, so not to worry.

A meditation practice can be established fairly quickly, although some people find meditation more difficult while others find it easy. If you find learning to meditate difficult, then my guidance for you would be to continue to do it until you feel you're doing it more easily. Learning to meditate and silence yourself is one of the initial steps in spiritual development that simply can't be skipped. If you're having trouble learning to meditate, perhaps look at it as the universe giving you the opportunity to get the hardest part out of the way first. You see, in meditation we can't hide from our true inner emotions and energies - good or bad. And if we find ourselves resisting meditation or having difficulty 'letting go' during meditation, then perhaps the meaning of this is that we have a lot of work to do - a lot of healing to achieve.

Begin meditating at least once a day at the beginning - even if it's for only ten or twenty minutes at a time. It's important to sit in the energy of meditation as often as you can at the beginning. As you become more accustomed to meditating, you'll find it easier and easier to do. But be sure that you're also doing 'emotional excavation', as I like to call it, in your meditation practice by continuing to ask spirit to show you something you need to know for inner healing. And then you must dig - dig deep within your being - and truly and honestly begin your own personal healing process.

Healing can take place through many avenues, and just as each person is unique, so too is the journey toward healing. Some healing modalities you might consider for your spiritual journey include Reiki, acupuncture, a spiritual advisor, or another type of professional therapist to talk to. Meditation, itself, is incredibly healing. But it's sometimes helpful to have someone else talk us through some of our journey to provide objective guidance. After all, some of the things that may come up during 'emotional excavation' might not be easy to face alone. So choosing a spiritual worker, a professional, or a close, trusted friend to assist through parts of our journey is likely a wise decision.

Remember: Helping others in their spiritual healing can't happen with significance unless you have navigated the healing journey, yourself. Your healing is the beginning of your spiritual unfoldment, and it's a sacred step. Allow yourself the time and attention you need on this most important part of your evolution and growth.

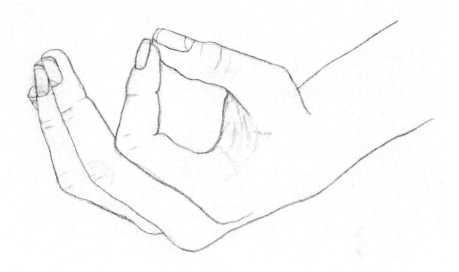

Part 2: Psychic Development Exercises

Following the first step of learning to silence yourself comes the learning of how spirit communicates with you (through site, through feeling, through colors, through sounds, etc.). It's also the starting point of building a spiritual or psychic dictionary, which includes signs, symbols, and references that spirit uses to communicate with you. These first aspects of psychic development form an integral part of the foundation of good mediumship work.

The following three exercises can and should be repeated often in the beginning of your development. They're designed to be done following a meditation of your choosing so that you are 'in the energy' before you start. And they're best done with at least one other person, but you can also try them alone. Either way, consider having someone read them aloud during the exercises so you remember what you're doing next, or become familiar enough with the exercises that you don't have to continue to check what to do next. Or if you're so inclined, you can record yourself reading the exercise and play is quietly while you are journeying through.

Before any work with spirit (including meditation), it's important to set your intention ahead of time. Know what you want to achieve, even if it's just relaxation or simply having an experience. It's also important to say some words (e.g., a prayer) that ask for protection from the Divine during the work you're undertaking. The following is a prayer I say prior to starting work with the spirit world.

Great Spirit, fill me with your light and your love. I ask for angels of protection to watch over me and protect this process. I ask to be a clear channel for loved ones today, and ask that my angels, loved ones, and guides only allow those being of the highest light and love near to me so the highest and best be served. Thank you.

I encourage you to modify this prayer into something that works for you. In your prayer, be sure to state what you're asking for (for protection and to be a clear channel), why you're asking for it (to serve the highest and best), and give gratitude (say thank you).

Exercise Example #1:
Meeting Our Main Spirit Guide

Begin your meditation as usual (guided or unguided). Nearing the end of the meditation, don't end it. Just stay in that energy for a moment. Take a look around you (with your third eye), and recognize that you're in the most beautiful place you've ever seen. Observe this place, feel it, love it. Enjoy it.

Now look off in the distance, and see a bright sphere of light moving toward you. As it comes nearer to you, the sphere becomes larger and larger. Finally it arrives in front of you, and it's no longer just a sphere of light. Look down, and see feet. Are there shoes on those feet? What do they look like? Now move your gaze upward. What clothing, if any, do you see? Hold your hands out now, and ask them to reach out to you. As they do, look up. See the face of this beautiful being of light who is here only for you. As you look upon them, imprinting their face in your memory, ask them their name. Even if it feels like you're making up what you're seeing, or what you're doing or hearing, just move through it - keep going. Stay in their energy for some time - you can expect to feel many emotions such as feeling loved, safe, and understood, and you'll likely want to stay in that energy for a long time.

Once you feel you're ready to move on, thank your spirit guide, and watch as they once again become a sphere of light moving away from you. Now conclude your meditation as usual.

This was your first meeting with your main spirit guide, and you may have learned their name (if you didn't, simply try again on another day). Be sure to use your spirit guide's name any time you wish to have them present, be it when you're down, alone, scared, need guidance, or feel you need spiritual protection. Also be sure to journal all of your early meditation experiences, as it's easy to forget some important information along the way.

It's well-believed in the spiritual community that we, as human beings, have many spirit guides, but we usually have one or two 'main' guides. For me, I recognize that I have one main spirit guide who's always with me. I feel that he never leaves. I also have other guides who seem to only be present during certain occasions or circumstances, and I like to think of them as more 'specialized' guides. For example, each time I have a beloved animal pass from this world to the next, I see one particular guide around me. I feel he's my guide that connects with the animals in my life and greets them at their transition. I have yet to learn his name, but I can recognize his face and stature.

Exercise Example #2:
Psychometry

Psychometry is the psychic ability to touch an object and receive imprinted information about it or from it.

This exercise requires working with at least one other person. More participants is even better. Begin your meditation as usual (guided or unguided). Throughout your meditation, ask spirit to work with you on the meaning of colors, and ask them to show you colors that correlate to or represent certain emotions. Give them examples of different types of emotions (happiness, sadness, fear, joy, etc.), and ask to be shown a color associated with each. When you feel you've gained new insight, complete your meditation, and record your experiences.

Once everyone has completed their meditation, have each person place something of theirs in a basket (keys, a piece of jewelery, a glove, etc.). Then, have everyone pick something out of the basket, blindly. Hold it in your hands, and ask spirit to show you emotion through color. Ask to see or feel what the owner of the item was feeling today. And ask to have a clue as to who the item belongs to.

Now each person can take their turn sharing the colors they saw, or the emotions they felt, and their guess of who the item belongs to. Compare the emotional information that came from the object with the item's owner. Did they feel those emotions today? I think you'll be surprised at how accurate this can be!

Also take special note of how you received the information from or about the item. Did you in fact see color, did you see an expression on someone's face, or did you feel an emotion inside of you as if it were your own? This will be your first clue into how spirit communicates with you most effectively.

Exercise Example #3:
Meeting Spirit

Once you've tried the first two exercise examples several times with success, and you're comfortable with meditating, it's time to move on to this third exercise. This exercise is best done with a group or at least one other person. It can be done on your own as well, but only as a matter of psychic exercise - you won't be able to validate any of your experiences with this exercise without someone else being present.

Before you begin this exercise, there are a few things that might happen, and I want you to be prepared so that you aren't frightened or uneasy. When we blend with spirit for the first time, or the first few times, it can sometimes feel overwhelming - even literally nauseating. Their energy and vibration is so vastly different than what we're used to feeling that we can often feel lightheaded, dizzy, tired, or nervous, and our hearts might beat strongly (or at least it feels that way). All of this is very normal. Even now when I channel a very strong loved one, I can feel lightheaded. But as we begin to channel the spirit's energy and pass their information along, it's like we're activating a pressure release valve. By giving life to their message, we are in effect releasing the energy that makes us feel overwhelmed or lightheaded. In preparation for this first meeting with the spirit world, be sure to stay seated. Don't plan on standing up - at least for a little while. And remember: You are safe and protected in the light of the Great Spirit - always. Spirit loved ones want you to work with them - you are meant to. So your first right in this work is to be ever-protected, and so you are.

Begin your meditation as usual. Nearing the end of your meditation, don't end. Stay in that energy for a moment. Now ask for spirit, a loved one of someone in the room with you, to come close to you. And now wait. Keep waiting. Don't expect to see anything, but rather stay open to however they might make themselves known to you. Wait for anything to come into your field of energy. Can you feel or see anything? Perhaps a wave or spark of light? What color is it? Or can you feel a new emotion or sensation? Is any part of your body tingling, like goosebumps, but you aren't cold? Or can you see a face? Just now, ask them to step even closer. And now what do you feel, see, or know? Try to sense or ask spirit about a few introductory things:

- Are they male or female (unless you can see them, in which case you may already know). If you can't see them, do you have an inkling of the spirit near you - like an inner knowing if they are male or female? If you can't pick up on this as an energy, ask spirit to either show you their face, or show you a symbol of male or female. Also remember, however, that spirit may reference their sex or gender, and of course biology and identity aren't always the same.

- What was their personality when they were here in the physical world? In response to this, they may have you hear a loud laugh, or you may feel very timid for a moment, or they may have you feel grumpy or withdrawn. Or perhaps they'll show themselves with one of their own typical facial expressions that tell a thousand words. However the information comes in, be open to receiving it.

- How did they pass from the physical world? In response to this, they may have you feel something in your own body, or they may show you an area of their own body that contributed to their passing. Alternatively, spirit may show you the scene of their passing in great detail, or they may send you a thought or word that describes the cause of their passing. Again, be open to any way the information might be communicated.

Thank spirit for stepping forward, and return to your regular awareness. You might think you'd like to accomplish more communication than this your first time encountering a loved one, but trust me, you'll likely be overwhelmed by the feeling of blending with spirit and may even forget these first three questions!

Be sure to write down all of the information you received from spirit. Did they show you their face as male or female, or did they make you know their identity in a different way? How did you know their personality - as an internal knowing or thought, or did they show you what looked like a movie reel playing a scene that depicted their personality? And when you learned how they passed from the physical world, did they make you feel something in your own body, did they show you something visually, or did you just know something that you didn't know before? Take note of all these things, and all the ways that spirit communicated with you. Understanding how spirit loved ones work with you will help you become more accurate, sooner.

By repeating this exercise many times, you'll be able to determine what your psychic strengths are. Are you mostly clairvoyant - do you see the best? Or do you feel or know best (clairsentient/claircognizant)? Or perhaps you hear most of what spirit's trying to communicate in the form of hearing an internal thought (clairaudient). While most Mediums have a significant strength in one of these ways of spirit communication, be open to the understanding that you're likely to receive information in all of these ways, and not just via the means you think you're best at.

After reading this part of the chapter, I'm going to leave you with this advice: Be patient. If the first time you attempt to blend with spirit nothing happens, simply try it again on another day. If you're meditating regularly, and progressing with meditation experiences, spirit will inevitably show up. So just wait for it. As I noted earlier, everything unfolding for you is happening at the pace that's just perfect for you - even if you don't think so. Unfortunately we can't argue with the universe on that!

Part 3: Raising Your Vibration

Once you've mastered the silencing of your internal dialogue (through meditation), and you've learned some of the ways that spirit communicates with you, you must learn to raise your vibration *without* going into a full meditation. Right about now you might be asking, "what the heck does raising your vibration mean?" Well, all things carry a vibration or level of energy, and this vibration or energy is generally governed by density. It's the physical vibration and the range of frequency of objects or people that allow our human senses to perceive them. If you can imagine the more dense an object is, the lower the frequency or vibration is. Further to this, imagine that spirit, something completely lacking in physical form and density, vibrates at a much higher frequency. So high, in fact, our regular five senses can't perceive them. And while we need to raise our vibration to connect with the other side, our loved ones have to lower theirs to such a level that we have even the faintest hope of sensing them.

Most people can intuitively sense vibration, but many are entirely unaware of what they're perceiving. A good example to illustrate our innate ability to sense and read energy can be found in the common scenario of walking into a room full with people at a party. Soon after entering, most people do an energetic scan of the personalities around them, and while most think they're just listening to words being spoken by other people, they're in fact sensing vibrational frequencies. And you will notice that based on how someone 'feels' to you, you will be attracted to them, or you will feel wholly uninterested.

It's important for me to note or state the obvious given the work that I do: Just because we can't perceive something with our regular five senses, doesn't mean or prove that it doesn't exist. An excellent example of this that I've heard many times is the dog whistle. If we blow the whistle, we (humans) don't perceive (hear) it. But we all know dogs can hear it!

The good news is that expanding our awareness (part of what happens in meditation) raises our vibration enough to perceive spirit. That's why when we're in a meditative state, it's much easier for us to see, hear, or feel spirit. So when starting out, it's best to meditate your way into connecting with the other side. But don't worry - once you become experienced at connecting in, you don't have to meditate for an extended period beforehand, if at all.

So let's talk about how to raise your vibration without going through a lengthy meditation. There are scores of techniques that can be used to raise your vibration, but I'll focus on what I use in practice. Note, however, that I use these techniques not because I was taught this way, but because they work for me and feel right. Similarly, my techniques are just a guide for you to start off on, and if something doesn't feel right, or doesn't 'ring true' for you, then try it differently. You are unique, and so your practice will never be exactly the same as someone else's.

For me, the preparation process for a reading takes about ten minutes before I'm ready to blend with spirit. I begin with a prayer. In my prayer, I ask divine energy to fill me with light and love, and I ask for angels of protection to watch over me. I also ask for the highest and best to be served, and I always finish with "Thank you". With my prayer, my intention is set, and I've raised my vibration some degree. Following my prayer, I visualize a chakra cleanse and balance in my own body, which is made complete with a grounding exercise at the root chakra and through the bottom of both my feet. The chakra cleanse, balance, and grounding exercise is fairly straightforward, and can be complimented with crystals or other tools. I don't regularly use any, but I have, and that's fine too.

Chakras are the energy centers in our body, and there are seven major ones aligned approximately along our spine. Each chakra corresponds to particular parts of our physical body, and also to particular parts of our consciousness. I highly recommend further learning related to the chakras, as understanding them is a vital part in working from a spiritual perspective.

very top and center of the head, visualize a violet or white-colored lotus flower opening slowly. See a beam of white light entering into the lotus through your crown and into your head from above, and say *Open to receive clearly*. The crown chakra represents our ability to be connected spiritually.

- At the sixth (third eye) chakra located between the brows, visualize an indigo-colored swirling circle. Imagine it expanding wider and wider. See the white light entering through your crown now reaching your third eye, and say *Open to see clearly.* The third eye chakra represents our ability to focus and see spiritually (including seeing spirit).

- At the fifth (throat) chakra located at the throat, visualize a sky-blue-colored swirling circle. Imagine it expanding ever-larger. See the white light reaching down in to the throat now, and say *Open to speak, listen, and interpret clearly.* The throat chakra represents communication and speaking our personal truths.

- At the fourth (heart) chakra located in the middle of the chest, visualize a green-colored swirling circle. Imagine it becoming larger and larger. The white light from above reaches down into the heart now. And say *Open to love and to feel clearly.* The heart chakra represents our ability to love and express compassion. For me, it's especially important to work at balancing and cleansing the heart chakra. A lot of people (non-Mediums) think the work we do filters through our head and out of our mouths. But in reality, like all spiritual healing practices, the work is being done through the heart. The information from above (from spirit) filters through the heart first.

- At the third (solar plexus) chakra located at the upper abdomen, visualize a yellow-colored swirling circle that expands quite large. The white light from the divine now reaches the solar plexus. Say *Open to confidence.* The solar plexus represents our ability to be confident and comfortable in ourselves. Ever been nervous for a performance, or maybe a test? Can't eat from nerves, stomach's unsettled, butterflies in your tummy (not the kind you get when you first fall in love...)? Those are all examples of your solar plexus being unsettled!

- The second (sacral) chakra is located in our lower abdomen, about two fingers below the navel. Visualize an orange-colored swirling circle here. As it becomes larger, the white light from above now reaches it. Say *Open to satisfaction and acceptance*. The sacral chakra represents abundance, wellness, and pleasure.

- At the first (root) chakra located at the base of the spine, visualize a swirling red-colored circle. As the chakra expands and the white light merges with it, say *Open to grounding*. From here, see roots sprouting from your first chakra and the bottoms of both your feet. Visualize these roots reaching deep, down into the earth. When they reach the center of the earth, they wrap tightly around a colored crystal (of your choosing) or a large rock or stone. The intention is that this practice keeps you grounded (in the physical plane) for the duration of your work. The root chakra represents foundation and being grounded.

Now visualize all of your chakras, from top to bottom, totally aligned and identical in size and shape, swirling in their respective colors and the white light from above. Complete three spiritual or diaphragmatic breaths (inhale into the belly and lower lung, working your way up to the mid and upper lungs, then exhale). And now you are ready to begin.

You might be wondering how during a spontaneous reading, when you have not 'prepared', you'll be able to perceive and communicate with spirit. Well here's the answer: As a human being with a spiritual practice, you will eventually and naturally begin to vibrate at a higher rate than someone who isn't keeping a spiritual practice—almost all spiritual practitioners do. So it will take very little effort, if at all, to blend with spirit at any old time.

CHAPTER 5
Signs, Symbols, and the Trust Factor

In addition to literal information, spirit uses signs and symbols to communicate with us. So you might ask yourself, "How do I know what symbols mean - how do I interpret them?" Well, for the time being, I'm going to help you with that. To begin, you really must use someone else's signs and symbols - whether they're from a teacher or a book. Otherwise, you may have no idea what spirit's showing you or trying to say. You may be able to see what they're showing, but in the absence of spirit showing you only literal things, you'll likely have no idea what it all means!

Signs and symbols are important to learn especially when spirit communicates with you visually (through your clairvoyant abilities). But what if you rely mostly on feeling, knowing, or hearing? How would signs and symbols help? Well, most Mediums use a combination of seeing, feeling, knowing, and hearing. Even Mediums who don't see actual spirit faces can still usually see images that spirit communicates. But if your strongest form of communication is something other than seeing, then you are likely to find spirit communicates with you using more literal information. For example, if you feel pain in your head when channeling a loved one, perhaps they're telling you they had brain cancer, a stroke, or perhaps Alzheimer's disease. If spirit wants to talk about a memory they shared with their loved one, they might have you recall a similar memory you have with your own family to make the connection. In these such cases, a visual dictionary might not be help-ful. But even using clairsentience, claircognizance, or clairaudience, spirit will still communicate information that could represent more than one meaning, so be sure to take note of all the possible meanings of one single piece of information. An example of this might be if spirit makes your legs tingle. It could mean they had issues with their legs and couldn't walk very well before they passed, or it could mean they had swelling in their legs from diabetes, or perhaps they only had one leg. Regardless of how you receive information from spirit, you will become better and better at un-derstanding what it all means with practice, and you are likely to find that the dictionary of items provided for you here is still useful.

I've developed my own psychic dictionary, which is constantly expanding. But at the beginning, I had to use someone else's until spirit began tailoring signs and symbols specifically for me. You, too, can expect that over time spirit will begin building your dictionary with you. You'll start to notice the same signs or sym-bols coming through during readings, over and over again. And you'll learn throughout your readings that these signs and symbols continue to have the same meaning. For example, I remember the first time spirit showed me clear tubing. As I was sitting with my client, I expressed to them that their loved one was showing me clear tubing that looked like either an oxygen or intravenous line. Then my client acknowledged that their loved one in fact was put on oxygen prior to their passing. Later that same week, another spirit loved one showed me the clear tubing again. I again expressed to my client what I was looking at, and they confirmed that their loved one in fact was hooked up to an intravenous line prior to their passing. So there it was - the formation of a new dictionary item. From that moment onward, when spirit shows me clear tubing, it's a symbol they were either hooked up to an intravenous or oxygen line prior to their passing.

As another example, my symbol for a loved one on the other side who knitted, crocheted, or sewed is a metal thimble. This was one of the first symbols I learned from spirit, directly. Several weeks in a row when I was a student, they showed me the thimble, and each and every time without exception, either the loved one in spirit or the client I was giving a reading for knitted, crocheted, or sewed.

Still there are Mediums, good ones, who don't use a dictionary. When they communicate with spirit, they interpret what they're feeling or seeing in literal terms, and they don't have 'standard' feelings or symbols that mean the same thing every time. You may well be the same, and that's okay. Either way, be open to however spirit communicates with you.

Before we move on, there's something I need to talk to you about: The trust factor. You can know all the symbols in the world that spirit might use to tell you something, but unless you trust the process and trust what they're communicating, you're never going to open your mouth and deliver their messages exactly as they are communicating them.

Learning to trust spirit is a process, and it doesn't happen overnight. You will experience many instances where you misinterpret something, or your client doesn't understand what you're talking about. Or your client may simply not remember at the time (which happens more often than you might think), or perhaps there's someone else in their life who can validate it. But regardless of the reason something doesn't make sense, if your client doesn't understand or can't validate something you're telling them, your confidence will be rattled. It's a sure thing in the beginning of learning mediumship.

Rattled confidence can make you hesitate to say exactly what spirit's communicating. You might choose to say something more generic rather than what they're specifically showing you because you're fearful you're going to be wrong, or that your client won't understand. Trust me when I tell you that you'll have this exact experience many times, and it's something you'll have to navigate on your own. Keep pushing through - keep experiencing and figuring things out. But remember...always give what you get, exactly how you get it. If you let this be your guiding rule when your trust is shaken, you'll do just fine. Trust me!

The Psychic Dictionary example provided next is by no means an exhaustive list but is meant to be a starting point. I've included some of the most common general references that spirit uses with me, which they may also use with you. Be sure to record any new signs or symbols that spirit presents to you, so that you can reference the meanings later and you won't forget what something means.

Psychic Dictionary

Pink Colored Light	Spirit person is sending love
Blue Colored Light	In need of healing, illness concern
Heat in the Face, Heart Pounding	Spirit person was very close to the sitter - not a distant relative
Blue Light Around a Body Part	Indicates an area of illness or trauma
Spirit Person Holding Chest (Female)	Illness in the heart, lung, or breast, or trauma in the chest
Spirit Person Holding Chest (Male)	Illness in the heart or lung, or trauma in the chest
Sense/Smell Smoke or See a Cigarette	A smoker
Hearing a Rattling Cough	Illness with the lungs and/or a smoker
Rocking a Baby	Someone had children, may have lost a child, or the sitter has lost a child
A Woman Standing in a Kitchen	Someone was a homemaker, took care of the family
A Person Hunched Over	Someone with issues with mobility, needed assistance or was very slow and/or actually was hunched over near the end of their life in the physical world
Thimble	Someone who knits, crochets, or sews
A Uniform	Someone who works in a blue-collared environment
White Shirt	Someone who works in a white-collared environment
Hands in Praying Position/A Rosary	A religious or spiritual person
Military Uniform	Someone who served in the military, police service, etc.
Feeling of Hitting a Brick Wall	Spirit person's passing was fast, sudden, and/or unexpected

Fingers Snapping	Spirit person's passing was fast, sudden, and/or unexpected
Female in Spirit Wearing Red Lipstick	Spirit person liked to look presentable and put-together, cared about their appearance
Religious Icons	A religious person
Clear Tubing	Spirit person had either an oxygen or intravenous line prior to passing/and/or was treated medically related to illness
Hospital Gown	Spirit person was treated medically before passing
A Hand on a Back	Spirit person supports an idea or decision
Person with a Heart Over Their Head	They are a spouse

Go through this dictionary a few times until you feel like you remember some of the sign and symbols, and begin asking spirit to use some of these signs and symbols with you. Also remember that the signs and symbols don't make up the full extent of how spirit communicates with us - a great deal of what they communicate is through literal information, and they'll use any number of ways to get that information across to us. For example, if spirit wants to communicate that they moved around a lot and never stayed in one place for long, they may do one of the following:

• SHOW you a person moving from one place to the next, never staying long

• Give you the FEELING of what it feels like to never be rooted, and to move from one place to the next

• Give you an internal KNOWING, in the same way that you know what your name is, that they moved around their whole life

- Have you HEAR a thought of something like "I moved a lot"

With all the ways that spirit can communicate with us, it can take work to determine what is a symbol, and what is literal information, and that's okay. If you need clarification from spirit regarding what they're showing you, just ask, and wait for the answer. If what spirit responds with is no more clear than it was before you asked for clarification, start by telling your client exactly what spirit is showing you or having you feel/know/hear. If they can't understand the information in literal terms, navigate what it could mean symbolically.

Psychic dictionaries are always expanding and changing, and so are our skills as Mediums in interpreting them. It's no secret that the longer you work with spirit and the larger your dictionary is, the more adept you'll be at bringing through not only a lot of information, but specific and unique information. If you find yourself without a symbol that you would like to have, simply ask spirit to make one for you. For example, if you don't have a symbol for a cancer connection related to a passing, ask spirit to use a shaved head as the symbol. Or you could ask them to show you a cancer ribbon if you prefer. The point is that we can make symbol suggestions too, and ask spirit to oblige, so don't be afraid to make the request!

CHAPTER 6
Creating an Opening Speech

Most Mediums only require the first name of a client before sitting with them, and I'm no exception (so you shouldn't be either!). Consider making it a point to communicate with prospective clients (perhaps through a website or social media page) that they shouldn't provide any details to you in advance about their life, or those in spirit. You might be surprised that, given the opportunity, many people will want to tell you their whole life story before you even begin a reading. But it's so important that they don't. If they tell you everything important about themselves, including who they have on the other side, then there is no more opportunity for you to GIVE THEM that information. Imagine this: If a client says to you, "I really want to connect with my Father, Ron, who passed from lung cancer three years ago," then you can no longer say to them, "I can feel a father energy around you, who references his lung area related to his passing, and he also acknowledges an R name." What would you or spirit be proving by saying that information after it was already divulged to you? Nothing. Except that you're a good listener! As much as possible, you want to be the one, as a Medium, providing the information about spirit.

Do encourage your prospective clients, however, to come prepared by knowing information about their loved ones in spirit (names, how they passed, other details about their life) so they can validate the information coming through. You see, mediumship is a three-way communication process (client, Medium, and spirit), and the more that your client can understand and acknowledge from spirit, the stronger the connection between you, the Medium, and spirit will be.

Mediums can't guarantee that one particular person in spirit will come through - spirit has their plan for what's taking place and who's coming through, and we can't change that. However, I always say to my clients that while it's not guaranteed, it generally is the case that the loved one they really want to hear from comes through. And I follow that up closely by saying that I believe when we communicate with spirit, we get what we need, and not necessarily what we want!

I prepare for a reading (through meditation and chakra balancing) before my clients arrive. But once they arrive, I don't just go straight into connecting with their loved ones. I start with an opening speech. Probably about half of my clients have never sat with a Medium before seeing me, so they sometimes have very little understanding of how mediumship readings work. My opening speech prepares them in a way.

You can put together whatever feels right for you, but I'll give you a basic example of my speech, out of which you may want to pick and choose parts to form your own speech.

My opening speech usually goes something like this:

As a Medium, I can't dictate who comes through from spirit. Spirit has their own plan for who's visiting, and I can't change that. However, most of the time we do hear from who we want to.

It's important to know that communicating with spirit isn't as simple as you and me sitting here talking. There are no conversations, no dialogue, no words, and no voices. If you hear me say "She's telling me this...", it's simply a presentation style - but generally no words are being spoken to me. Spirit will show me things, have me feel things, know things, or hear things in the form of an internal thought, and it's my job to interpret what those things mean and present them to you. But you are still part of this process. The more you can understand and validate from them, the stronger my connection will be. So please allow yourself to be emotional and vulnerable, because it will make this experience much more meaningful.

Most of the time, it's our family and our friends who come through from the other side. But on occasion you can have someone connected to you in a different way come through. For example, if you have a colleague at work, a friend, a sister-in-law who lost someone, this is fair game for those loved ones in spirit to come through to give a message to them. But not to worry, because if someone like that does come through, you won't be able to validate very much about them and we won't stay with them long.

I also talk to my clients about mediumship on television. I usually let them know that I believe most mediumship on TV is genuine, but I also let them know that some of the shows are of course edited so as to showcase only the very best points throughout a reading. And unfortunately, the edited shows don't seem to show parts of readings where the client doesn't understand a reference from spirit. But we all know that it happens. If you've ever watched live, unedited, public mediumship, you'll see that it can and does happen that Mediums bring through validation from spirit that doesn't make sense to the person receiving the reading. Of course this happens because mediumship isn't a perfected process. We can't fully define or understand it, so naturally there can be points during readings, public or private, where the communication might be imperfect.

The point in talking about mediumship on TV is to address expectations that might arise from watching it, and to let your clients know that it's normal if something comes from spirit that they can't place right away. In my experience, if something in a reading doesn't make sense or can't be validated, it can usually be placed at a later time when someone remembers something they've forgotten or when someone else in their life can validate it for them.

One other thing to make note of - make sure to notice if your client crosses their arms or legs prior to or during your reading. From an energetic viewpoint, this says "I'm not open". And trust me when I tell you that's exactly what's communicated to the spirit world, and you'll find spirit has immense difficulty in working with you if their loved one here in the physical is 'closed off'.

A client has never sat in front of me without spirit accompanying them. However, with spirit there are no hard and fast rules, and nothing is impossible. If that were to happen to you (beforehand during your preparation, nothing from spirit comes forward, or as your client sits in front of you, nothing happens), my advice would be to consider it like this: If spirit doesn't come forward for someone, there are probably only two reasons for that. The first and most likely would be that it's not part of their journey to hear from their spirit loved one yet. For whatever reason, it's part of your client's plan to travel through this particular part of their life without connecting with their loved ones in spirit. And that doesn't mean they're left to walk their immediate path on their own with no divine guidance. They always, always, always have instant access to their guardian angel and their main spirit guide, and of course the Great Spirit, also known by a multitude of other names to many - such as God, Goddess, Universe, etc. We have a whole team of helpers on the other side that we're intimately connected with, all the time.

The second possible explanation for no one in spirit stepping forward could be that your client truly has no one on the other side with whom they had a legitimate and genuine relationship with. This may sound strange - why would someone visit a Medium if they've never lost someone close to them? Well, some people just want to experience sitting with a Medium - some just for an experience, others perhaps with different motives, like to trip you up or challenge your ability. Either way, I would expect this to be a rare occurrence, but one that is at least possible. In these such cases, be sure to follow your gut, and ask you spirit helpers to guide you through the experience in a tactful and loving way.

I mentioned earlier that who we hear from in spirit is usually who we want to hear from. But that isn't always the case. I believe we hear from who we need to hear from - whether we want to hear from them or not. However, as with most things, the time people spend with a Medium is limited - usually an hour, maybe less, maybe a little longer. Now imagine it's you sitting with a Medium, and you have several loved ones in spirit who want to connect with you. Imagine there's a 'line up' that your spirit people are making to blend with the Medium. The Medium will start with the person who gets their attention first. If that person happens to be your sweet grandma, who loves you very much, she might stay with the Medium for 20 minutes or more. So now you've got 40 minutes left, and you still haven't heard from Mom. Next person stepping forward is Dad. He loves you so much, you've never heard from him since his passing, and he's got a lot to say. By the time Dad gives you his messages, you've got 10 minutes left. Just then, your old childhood dog runs past, and the Medium starts describing the dog to you. Before you know it, your time is up, and you hadn't heard from Mom. Does that mean Mom wasn't there? Perhaps, but most likely not. If Mom was further back 'in line' (by virtue of her personality being more timid, perhaps), then she simply didn't get her chance to come forward because of the limited time the Medium was working with.

So how can we help our clients avoid this type of thing happening? Well, there's a technique for connecting with specific loved ones in spirit that's worth mentioning. Most Mediums are aware of this, even though in my experience, it doesn't need to be used all that often. This technique is called 'calling by name', and utilizing this tool is sometimes the only legitimate way to avoid your client not getting a chance to hear from someone particular in spirit, assuming the spirit person is, in fact, there and ready to connect. I usually say to my clients something like this:

In my experience, it usually happens that more than one loved one comes through during a session. So the first person you hear from may not be the one person you'd really like to hear from. So what we can do is if about half way through your session you still haven't heard from that one person, we can try calling them by name.

How it works is I will notice the most persistent spirit, by virtue of their personality or the importance of their message. But that doesn't mean there aren't other loved ones behind them 'in line'. So calling by name allows me to ask the forward spirit to step aside and allows the person we are calling, if they are there, to bypass the 'lineup', and come right to the front.

Just the same as the fact that I've never sat with a client and not had spirit step forward, I have also never called by name and not had that exact spirit person step forward. But if it ever happens to you that the person you call doesn't step forward, I would provide the same explanation as I already mentioned - that it's simply not part of their journey to hear from that particular loved one yet.

CHAPTER 7
The Framework of a Reading

Can you remember from your primary or elementary school days learning the 'order of operation' in mathematics? Well, similar to that, a good mediumship reading has a general order to it. It's something you might have noticed if you've ever sat for more than one mediumship reading.

An evidential mediumship reading is generally made up of two parts: Part one is the presentation of the evidence, or the validating information that spirit brings forward. Part two, which is usually much shorter in duration when compared to part one, is messages. Messages are meaningful pieces of guidance, advice, or expression that may or may not be validating but are meant to reach the hearts of the message's recipients.

Remember: Anyone can say "I have your mother stepping forward, and she's saying she loves you". It may be real mediumship taking place, but nothing is proven in saying what I've just quoted. Evidential mediumship is providing unique and specific information from and about the person in spirit - typically things that people would describe as information the Medium couldn't know unless they were in genuine communication with a deceased loved one. Evidential mediumship is what I practice, and it's what I'm teaching you in this book.

There are some basic pieces of information that, as a Medium, you should be obtaining from spirit and presenting to your client or sitter in each and every reading you give. Not only is there specific information you'll need to ask spirit, but there is also a general order in which to do it.

In using the order of questions I'm about to give you, you'll be presenting information (proof that you're communicating with a unique loved one on the other side) to your client in a way that keeps confusion at bay, and in a way that will help them recognize right away which of their loved ones you're bringing through. As your experience grows, you might wish to enhance the list of questions or change the order, but while you're learning, "stick to the program", as my Dad would say! Spirit will soon learn what questions you're going to ask and when, and at some point, you'll no longer need to ask the questions at all - they'll just give you the answers before a word comes out of your internal voice. It's like this: Have you ever been to the same coffee shop, day after day ordering the same double-double coffee, and then one day, the person working at the counter no longer asks you for your order because they already know what it is? Well, it's the same for spirit. At some point, they no longer have to wait to hear what your questions are - they already know!

Before we move into the question framework of a reading, it's important to talk about the language of a reading. What do I mean by that? Well, it's important when we're relaying what spirit's communicating that we use appropriate or accurate wording. For example, if spirit steps forward and you feel the energy of someone who was quiet, reserved, or conservative, then consider describing that information in this way: "I FEEL their personality is a little on the quiet side". Or if spirit shows you a small dog they are connected with, say "She is SHOWING me a small dog that she loved very much." Another example might be if spirit sends you an audible thought of a name, you might say "I'm HEARING the name Betty". The point here is to use a variety of words to describe how spirit's communicating with you (seeing, feeling, hearing, smelling, etc.), because not only is it accurate with respect to how they're communicating with you, it also adds dimension to what you're saying. Try to avoid saying "I see". For example, rather than saying "I see a large blue vehicle", instead say "She's showing me a large blue vehicle". This helps your client understand that what you're seeing is coming from spirit and not just from your psychic sight.

Information to Obtain from Spirit, in Order

1. Are they male or female in terms of gender or identity?

2. Are they young, old, in between?

3. What's their physical appearance?

4. How did they pass from the physical world?

5. What was their personality like?

6. What hobbies/interests did they have?

7. What did they do for work?

8. What is a shared memory between them and their loved one here?

9. Is there a momento they left behind?

10. What are some special dates to acknowledge (birthday, anniversary, when someone passed, etc.)?

11. What are some special names to acknowledge (theirs, someone in the family, a special pet, etc.)?

12. What is something they've seen your client do recently or since their passing (this proves to your client that their loved one still exists and is a part of their life - seeing what they are doing and supporting them in their life)?

13. Messages they wish to share (why have they stepped forward?)

When you first start giving readings, be sure to write down spirit's answers. Always have a pen and paper with you while you're preparing for your reading and during it. Often times during the preparation for a reading, spirit will start sending information to you that you may forget by the time your client arrives.

There are plenty of other questions you can ask spirit during a reading, and you can be as detailed as you feel comfortable with. But at a minimum, you should aim to ask and receive answers for most, if not all, of the thirteen questions above. If all you get are the answers to these questions, it should be enough information that your client is confident you're communicating with their unique loved one in spirit. And even if they can't understand some of the answers, or you simply get something wrong, that's okay. The goal is to get the majority of the information correct, and you'll know throughout the reading whether or not your client feels enough correct information has been presented.

Another important note is to never finish your reading on a 'no' answer from your client. For example, if you're nearing the end of your reading and are about to move to messages, make sure the last thing you said to your client in the validation portion wasn't something they didn't understand. If it was, go back to spirit and ask another validating question, and don't move on to messages until the last validation made absolute, clear sense to your client. It's so important that you do your best to leave your client feeling confident and faithful that their loved one in spirit is really present.

You might want to ask some of these additional questions once you feel comfortable with the information exchange between you and spirit:

- How long ago did they pass?
- How old were they?
- What did their house look like?
- What did the day of their funeral/memorial look like?
- Were they buried, cremated, or other?
- How many people make up their family?
- Who are they with on the other side?

You will also find that with the more readings you do, spirit will give you much more information than just the questions you're asking. And please allow them to do that - some of the most important information they want you to share with their loved one here will be in the communication that isn't in response to a question. If spirit communicates something to you without your asking, deliver that information in the same way you would an answered question. You may not have context to what spirit's saying, but deliver it all the same. As an example, you might say, "Your sister is showing me lace curtains in no context whatsoever - can you understand what this means?"

Finally, always finish the validation part of your reading with an open floor for spirit. Consider saying to the spirit loved one, "Is there anything else you'd like to say?" And then wait. If something comes, great. If not, then you've done your job in honoring and representing the spirit person you're working with.

CHAPTER 8
What if Nothing Makes Sense?

In an ideal situation, spirit will respond to your questions directly - meaning, you ask, "what is something your loved one still has of yours?", and they will answer with one of those things. But unfortunately, it doesn't always work that way! Communicating with spirit isn't a perfected process, and it isn't entirely definable, which is why any Medium, no matter how good or experienced, can be met with a client who doesn't understand something from spirit. Wouldn't it be amazing if every spirit loved one would right away give irrefutable evidence like their first, middle, and last names, their address, phone number, license plate, exact date of birth, death, etc.? Wouldn't it?! I think we all wish it worked that way, but alas, it doesn't.

Instead of answering your questions directly, spirit may give you an answer to a question other than the one you're asking. For example, if you ask spirit to show you a memento of theirs, they may respond by showing you a number of things. For this example, let's use a pearl necklace. So you say to your client "She's showing me a pearl necklace - do you have something like that of hers?" What happens if your client says no? Well, there are a couple of options.

If your client doesn't recognize something you're bringing through from their loved one, it may simply be a matter of incorrect context. Let's go back to the pearls - if your client can't recognize them as something belonging to their spirit loved one that they now have, try proposing what spirit's showing you in a different way. For example, "If you can't recognize the pearls as belonging to them, can you understand them in a different way? Did she have pearls that *someone else you know* might have of hers?" Your client may end up making the connection in a different way than you expect, which is perfectly fine. They may end up connecting the pearls with something completely different than the context in which you asked spirit that initial question. For example, they might let you know that their husband just recently bought a string of pearls for them, and in this case, spirit is showing you something they've seen happen in their loved one's life recently. And again, that's perfectly fine.

While we're on the topic of spirit showing pearls, I remember a reading I gave over the phone for a mom and sister. Their session was a beautiful reunion with their amazing son and brother who they lost tragically just a few months prior. At the end of their session full of compelling validation and lovely messages, their son and brother showed me a string of pearls, but not in any context. He was holding the pearls up in the air. So I said, "He's showing me pearls. Just pearls. Can you understand a connection with him and pearls?" To my heart's and spirit's content, the mother gasped. She said her nickname was "Pearly", and that prior to her reading she said to her self if her son mentioned Pearly, she'd know it was him. How wonderful!

As your experience builds, you'll learn how to navigate the waters of making sense of context. You'll also find that as time goes on, and you have more and more readings under your belt, a huge amount of information given to you from spirit will have the context very clearly communicated. And in some other cases, there will be no context at all, and that's okay. Like most things, becoming familiar, experienced, and good at giving a mediumship reading is a process - so stick with it!

Misinterpretation of what spirit's saying can certainly happen at any time. After all, communicating with other side isn't a perfected process, so no matter how experienced you are, no matter how accomplished your are, things may come up in a reading that you or your client doesn't understand. Most the time, however, those things that can't be validated during the reading can be validated later (either by your client remembering something they couldn't during the reading, or by someone else in their life).

I receive emails and phone calls all the time from clients who had one or two things come up during their reading they couldn't place straight away, only to remember something on their drive home or have someone else in their life give the validation. I remember one client who sat for a lovely reading with me one afternoon, and something came up in her reading that she couldn't place. I was channeling her paternal grandmother, and clear as day, grandma was showing me a refrigerator. She had me know, internally, that the refrigerator was in her kitchen (in a place she used to live), and that this fridge connected with her son in some way. As I navigated through context with no avail to my client understanding, I simply said to her, "You can't understand this, and I can't change what grandma is saying. She's showing me there's a refrigerator connected to her and your dad, so please ask your dad if he can understand it." That same afternoon, my client sent an email telling me about her dad's response to the question. As it turned out, grandma was on point even though it didn't make sense at the time! Sometime before her grandma passed, my client's dad was asked to move grandma's fridge in the kitchen where she lived. He struggled with moving it, and in frustration, threw it across the lawn! What a very specific memory to recall!

So sometimes, no matter how you try, you won't be able to understand context, and again, that's okay. One thing I see often with new or learning Mediums is the tendency to give quite a lot of information with no context. So rather than sticking to a general order of information exchange, and doing their best to understand context, they allow spirit to simply give them information in any order, in any way, and at any time. And the problem with this is the client can't follow along, and they have to do a lot of work to understand even one single piece of information. Remember, non-Mediums generally don't understand how spirit communication works, and they shouldn't have to do the brunt of the work to understand the message - that's your job! If you find spirit is continually giving you information in no context, or you frequently can't understand context, it's likely an indication that more mediumship practice is needed. So just view it as a challenge to sharpen your budding skills!

You might find on occasion that a client feels particularly closed. They may cross their arms as soon as they sit with you, and their energy may feel like 'I don't want to be here, and I'm not going to believe it anyway'. There will always be clients like that, and you're sure to find that no matter how much concrete, solid validation you give them, it will never be enough. Their energy or demeanor will leave you feeling unsatisfied, and you'll feel like you need to keep going to get that *one thing*, that one piece of information from spirit that will break their wall down. But you know what? It will probably never come, and you might feel like you didn't do your job. And that's okay. Believe it or not, not everyone who sits with you is actually ready or willing to start the spiritual growth that can come out of learning that we are eternal. They might not be ready to know that death as we know it - as the end of existence, the end of relationships, the end of reciprocated emotion - is a lie.

Now we've talked about how spirit communicates - through sight, feeling, emotion, inner knowing, thoughts, hearing (either as in internal thought or an audible sound). But there is another way that spirit can get information to us...they can do it in a physical way. What does that mean? Well, I'll give an example to illustrate. Some time ago I was giving a reading to a client, and my hands became very itchy - I couldn't stop scratching them no matter what I did! I had no reason to be so itchy, and I was perfectly fine before we (my client and I) sat together. So I asked if they could understand this constant itching in relation to their loved one coming through (their mom in this case). I was absolutely delighted for them to confirm that their mother had fairly serious eczema, and was itchy all the time. And wouldn't you know it that as soon as my client acknowledged it, the itching stopped! Amazing. So, if you find yourself moving a certain way, saying words in a different way than usual, or perhaps feeling something in your body that you're certain doesn't 'belong' to you, be sure to ask your client if they can understand it connected to their spirit loved one.

I always say there are generally two reasons why spirit steps forward. The first is to prove that they still exist - that when we pass from the physical world, we aren't just dead and gone. We are souls first. And steps one through twelve from the Information To Obtain From Spirit in Chapter seven are what provide spirit and you, as a Medium, the opportunity to prove it. The second reason why spirit steps forward is to give their loved ones here in the physical world advice and guidance from their all-knowing and loving perspective on the other side.

I've said it before, and I'll say it again: The combination of validation and messages serves as proof of the continuation of life after physical death, and demonstrates that we are never alone - that our connection of love still exists!

Now is a good time to begin practicing on as many friends, relatives, and strangers as you can. Sometimes practicing on people we know well can be difficult because we know so much about them. For example, it's not validating if spirit comes through with information about three children if you already knew your sitter (the person receiving the reading) has three kids. For that reason, strangers are usually best. But as you're learning, friends and family are usually the most forgiving of your mistakes!

If you've joined a development circle (online or in-person), then sitters will likely be provided for you, so that takes a lot of work out of trying to find people to practice on. Now, it may seem strange to be part of an online development circle because you're doing virtual readings - that is, you're not physically in the same place as your sitter. But I can tell you that on the other side, time and space are not linear as we perceive them here, and from a mediumship perspective, there's no difference when working remotely or in-person. My wonderful telephone and e-mail clients (and I) can attest to that!

CHAPTER 9
Maintaining a Spiritual Practice

In comparison to teachers, workshops, books, and the like, spirit is the best teacher of all things spiritual - bar none. But no matter how many readings you give in your life, maintaining your spiritual practice beyond just 'giving readings' is so important.

Even though it's safe to say each encounter with spirit is worthy of being considered a learning moment, enriching and expanding our awareness through new and different experiences is invaluable. On a soul level, our continuous evolution and growth can only enhance our connection with the spirit world, and make us better Mediums.

Some of the most healing and growth-filled experiences I've had on my spiritual path have come through working with other practitioners. For example, some of my peak growth experiences came out of activities like Past Life Regression and Life Between Lives Regression.

Before I talk about Past Life Regression and Life Between Lives Regression, I'll refresh you on the differences between a spirit and a soul. The soul can be defined as our whole or higher self, and it experiences many lifetimes in its journey toward spiritual perfection. In comparison with the spirit, I'll reiterate the analogy of the orange slice: The soul is represented as an orange - a whole orange, made up of many slices. The orange slices are the many aspects, or incarnations of the soul, called spirits. So my soul, the whole orange, resides in the spirit world (though it's ever-connected and one with my spirit here on earth). But the slice of the orange, the spirit here experiencing this incarnation, is Mary-Anne.

During Past Life Regression, we're given the opportunity to recall other aspects of our soul, or other spirit incarnations of it. During my first Past Life Regression, I recalled the soul memory of being a young boy named Johnny. Just as I, Mary-Anne, am a spirit that makes up part of my soul, so too is Johnny a spirit that makes up part of my eternal self - my soul. During that particular lifetime, my point of passing, or the point at which I died in that lifetime, was a traumatic memory. I was a young boy - no more than eight or nine years old. I was sickly my whole life, and my mother rarely let me outside. She was my lifeline, and sole caregiver - she was everything to me in that lifetime. On the day I passed from that life, I was in the kitchen of our small wooden house, looking out at my mom through the kitchen window.

I could see her - she was hanging clothes on a line, and stumbling over chickens at her feet. I so desperately wanted her to hear me, but I had no more than a whisper come out of my diaphragm. I began feeling like I was spinning, like I was in a centrifuge, and I knew I was dying. But I didn't want to be alone. A few minutes passed and my little body in that lifetime fell to the floor, and not a moment later I was literally outside of my body. I recalled seeing the faces of loved ones, my ancestors, and their greeting gave me great peace. I wanted to go with them, and I no longer felt anguished being separated from my mom.

A few months later I had my second experience with Past Life Regression. This time I visited a lifetime where I was a mother of two young children. My point of passing in this lifetime was also distressing - probably even more-so than my life as Johnny. This time, I died while trying to save my two children. I was in a small village with my family, and was carrying both my babies on my hips when a large cavalry stormed through. They stopped at nothing as they rode, and mere seconds before they were to crush us, I threw my babies into a canvas hut. They survived, but I was trampled and died savagely.

I wasn't surprised in the least that spirit had me recall these particular lifetimes. I made the connection right away between those past life experiences and the fear I held for my daughter losing me, and that connection helped me to understand part of the reason I had those fear emotions in the first place. More importantly, I recognized on a conscious and subconscious level that I had no basis for holding that energy of fear in my current lifetime. In the days and weeks that followed my past life experiences, my life changed. You see, I had these experiences fairly early on in my spiritual development, and I still suffered from anxiety of leaving my daughter. Slowly but surely, the grip of anxiety and fear lessened, and it continued to do so until it held on by a mere thread. And then one day, it let go of me entirely - or should I say I let go of it? My past life experiences in conjunction with my meditation practice, acupuncture, energy healing, and working with spirit were the pieces to my puzzle of wellness. When we understand on a fundamental level that physical death isn't the end of our loving relationships, we become freed from the burden of the fear of death. Learning that we exist on a greater level than a physical body, and knowing that to be the truth, unequivocally, is so very healing.

During Past Life Regression, we journey, under hypnosis, into lifetimes our soul has lived prior to this current incarnation. There are other ways to tap into or experience some of our past lives, such as through a psychic who can access your energetic history. But this type of experience is vicarious - meaning your aren't directly experiencing or remembering anything first-hand. Rather, someone is telling you what their insight is. This isn't to discredit having a vicarious past life experience, because there's certainly learning value in it. But the greatest learning and healing opportunities do more often than not come through first-hand experiences.

In Past Life Regression, we are afforded the opportunity to access the origins of many issues that might affect us in this lifetime - some of which seem to have no basis or reason for existing in our life. Past life regression therapists will tell you that powerful emotions, patterns, and thoughts that are experienced in past lives may manifest in this incarnation in other forms such as fears, phobias, allergies, illnesses, and relationship hurdles.

Revisiting the origins of old emotions or patterns, through the unconscious mind, helps us to release old energetic patterns and heal. The goal of Past Life Regression is to provide us an understanding of the soul's memory in order for us to release, forgive, and grow, and it gives us a better understanding of who we are, as a soul.

Life Between Lives Regression is an equally fascinating and important part of spiritual growth and healing. Similar to Past Life Regression, Life Between Lives Regression is experienced under hypnosis, and the unconscious mind is accessed. During the regression, you recall the soul memory of the time you spent on the other side in between your last lifetime and this one.

One of the purposes of Life Between Lives Regression is to gain insight and understanding of your current life plan (the plan you designed for yourself), as well as your life purpose/s. It's a truly incredible experience where you're afforded many delights, such as meeting and communicating with your main spirit guide, your soul group (the group of souls you incarnate with over and over again), reuniting with passed loved ones, just to name a few! Other experiences or practices important to me in maintaining my spiritual practice include things that heartily nourish my soul. Aside from wonderful activities that I regularly engage in like spiritual retreats, gatherings, meditation, and experiencing nature, I also do purely mundane things that hold tremendous value in my heart. For me, I ride horses - I spend time with one of my many earth angels - my sweet horse, Ralphie. Time spent with him is like no other. After our time together, I feel full to the brim with love and satisfaction. I also birdwatch. Birdwatching (or birding) brings a level of excitement and enjoyment to my life that no human interaction has yet to bring - a true sign that the activity is one of my 'soul foods'! If something feels good, and you love it, do it as often as you can. When we have soul-level experiences like Past Life Regression or other types of healing, it gives us first-hand knowledge of spirit's nature, and therefore our nature, as we too are spirits.

Self-exploration and understanding of your own soul further prepares you to work in service to others and the divine by bridging the connection between here and the hereafter. Simply stated, you must have gained your own knowledge, understanding, and wisdom in order to share any with someone else. When you're whole, when you're healed or healing, then you can help others do the same. So it makes sense then, that the greatest healing work you can do is for yourself. Because it's your own experiences with healing, soul-level awareness and growth that uniquely qualify you to assist others on a similar journey.

CHAPTER 10
Limits, Boundaries, and Shutting Down

It was important for me to establish boundaries with spirit as soon as I began working with them. I concluded that if I worked with spirit, I wanted to be comfortable - all the time. I never wanted to be made uncomfortable or fearful. I also knew that I only ever wanted to work with spirit that walked in the light, and radiated the highest light and love. I noted earlier that my practice doesn't include things like spirit rescue, or house and personal clearings from lower energies (energies that don't embrace or exist in pure divine light and love). I don't practice these things because I don't feel they're part of the work I'm meant to do - at least at this point in my life. As I said, there are plenty of practitioners who are very good at this type of work, and I know at least one of them that is quite exceptional... so I send anyone who comes to me with these types of matters to her! And I'm delighted to do so, as, unlike me, that type of work is part of her soul's journey.

Places hold vibrations and energy imprints of events that have taken place there over time, and while many places hold exceptionally high vibrations (like Sedona,

Arizona, for example), sometimes places hold vibrations that are lower (think old battlefields in Europe - if you're sensitive to energy, you can feel the memory of what's taken place in those locales). Similar to the vibration or energy of places having the capacity to be lower, spirit person energy can be lower, too. On occasion I'll pick up on energy that may have a lower vibration. And when it happens, I simply choose to ignore it and give it absolutely no attention. Sometimes it takes a bit of time before the lower-energy spirit person gets my drift, but the energy always eventually moves on and away from me. On occasion, I have chosen to remove myself from a place because of overwhelming lower energy, which can be uncomfortable on many levels if you're sensitive to energy. Follow your intuition, as I do, to know whether you should stay in a space, or move on.

If you find yourself in the presence of a spirit energy that doesn't feel 'warm and fuzzy', you will have to choose what your response is going to be. You can choose to ignore and not engage. However, if you feel it's in your path to work with assisting these types of spirit people toward the light, then my recommendation is that you work with an experienced practitioner who can teach how to safely work with lower energies.

I have several boundaries and limitations established with spirit. One of the very first that I communicated to the spirit world was that I don't want see spirit people with my waking eyes. When spirit communicates with me, they are very much visual. But I've expressed that my boundary on visual is to see mostly with my mind's eye (or third eye). Really, I don't want to be walking to the bathroom in the middle of the night and see someone walk past me in the dark - who would?!

Another limitation I was sure to let spirit know from the beginning was that I never want to have my children or animals be startled or disturbed by them. Their sense of well-being is as important to me as my own, and explaining what spirit people are to children and animals isn't that easy! If you have young children or animals, you may want to consider this as a limitation for yourself as well.

Mediums are often asked about "shutting down" or "turning off". Sometimes Mediums openly say they never shut down - that they can't - that they're always connected with the spirit world and never have a moment of rest. So no matter where they go or what they're doing, they see and feel spirit. But for me (and for a lot of other Mediums), I operate on a switch, if you will. I go grocery shopping, eat at restaurants, go to dinner parties, and I am not inundated with spirit. But if I want to, I can simply choose to turn on my switch, and I can begin connecting with spirit world energies. This is the way I like it - it works for me, and makes my life fairly normal most of the time!

Still, there is one time of day that usually proves difficult to manage when it comes to seeing spirit. For me, it's when I lay down for bed - of course! How convenient! When I lay down, relax, and close my eyes, I will usually see faces of people - not people that I know. They're often just looking back at me, and I try to shift my focus away from their faces, because it's not my desire to connect. This is when I begin my 'shutting down' technique.

To start, I imagine a golden door at the top of my head (at my crown chakra), and visualize it slamming shut. I then lock the door with a key, and place that key within my glowing green heart chakra for safe keeping. I'll then say a prayer to my guardian angel asking for peaceful sleep and protection.

Over time I learned my shutting down technique works about half the time, and the other half it just doesn't. When it doesn't work, I usually pray to my angels and spirit guides, and I imagine something lovely in my mind - usually my horse, cantering around a perfectly groomed sand-ring, and the ride is comfortable as a couch. Then usually, before I know it, I'm asleep.

I think it's important to establish a shutting down practice. While it's beautiful and amazing to be connected with the universe and spirit, we also have to function as human beings in the physical world, and sometimes if we're very deeply connected to spirit all the time, it can be difficult. For example, imagine sitting in a high profile meeting giving a presentation on a new product line your company just launched. Now imagine during the presentation, your new business client's dearly departed mom won't move out of your sight line because she really wants to get a message to her daughter. Could you imagine? In that situation, I bet you'd wish you had learned to shut down!

In all seriousness, it's important to know how to limit or close your connection to the spirit world, so my advice is to make it a point to learn what works for you. Shutting down or grounding is an especially good practice after a giving a reading to a client or having a spiritual experience. For me, I'll eat something and do fairly mundane things like clean up the kitchen or kids' toys, watch the television, or talk to someone about non-spiritual things. These types of activities help ground us to earth, and shift our awareness from the spiritual to the physical.

Spirit has made themselves known to me at so many inopportune or inappropriate times, and the same is likely to happen to you. And it will be up to you to know what is or isn't an inappropriate time to pass along a message. For example, I remember being at my husband's Granny's funeral, and I could see and hear Granny, clear as day. She had a message she wanted me to pass along to a couple of her children. But even though her children knew I was Medium, I never told them what she wanted to say. I waited for a time that was less difficult for them - for a time when their grief was a little lighter. I would encourage you to assess a situation before you pass along messages from spirit, and if you aren't sure, then wait. You don't want to be in a situation where a message or validation from the other side makes someone here overwhelmed or uncomfortable. If it happens that spirit steps forward but you aren't prepared to pass along the message, simply thank them for stepping forward and let them know you won't be able to pass it along at this time. You can even ask them to create another opportunity down the road for the message to be shared, and if it's really important, they'll likely make it happen.

CHAPTER 11
Giving Healing Through Mediumship

Creating a spark of hope in someone - hope their dearly departed still exist - is something of exceptional beauty. When clients leave their sessions with me knowing their loved ones live on, albeit in a different way, my work is done. I can tell you from experience when someone visits a good Medium at the right time in their grief or in their life, the most wonderful and magical healing can take place.

Of all the wonderful gifts that are mediumship, one thing connecting with spirit loved ones can't do is replace the process of grieving. In fact, sitting with a Medium during the early stages of grief might not make anyone feel any better or different. Whether we know they exist in another way or not, nothing can change the fact that we still have to go through the process of learning to live without them here in the physical world. All the validation in the world doesn't change the fact that we just want them here with us in the same way they were before.

Everyone is an individual and grieves and grows at their own pace. Healing is a very personal journey, and the right time to sit with a Medium won't be the same for everyone. I've met many people who benefited so significantly from communicating with a loved one soon after a passing. And I've also seen mediumship be much more meaningful for someone after having begun the process of healing and steered out of the thick of shock and disbelief that their loved one is no longer here.

One of my most memorable readings was with a young widow, who for all intents and purposes shouldn't have been sitting with me for a reading. I was traveling home from vacation with my family, and on our way I was checking emails while my husband was driving. I had a reading request from a young woman who was hoping to meet before returning to England a few days later. I replied immediately that I wouldn't be able to meet with her since my waiting list was several months long, and with just coming home from vacation, I had about a million-and-one things to do when we got back. I sent the response, and no sooner than I pressed the send button did my daughter say to me, "I can see a red light, mummy. Like an angel light, but a red one". Just then I became flushed with heat, which is a sign spirit uses with me to convey intense love. I knew instantly someone was trying to get my attention from the spirit world, and I determined it was connected to the woman who I'd just responded to.

Before she had a chance to reply, I sent another email letting her know I would try my best and to stay tuned. I said to spirit, "If I need to meet with this woman, you need to make it happen." With all we had to do when we got home to unpack and get settled after vacation, I was sure my husband wouldn't be keen on watching our two kids shortly after arriving home. But not surprisingly, spirit worked their magic, and he was happy to accommodate this impromptu reading. So we made arrangements to meet two days later.

You see, she had lost her husband in a tragic horse-back-riding accident just a few weeks earlier, and she was desperate to connect with him before heading back to England where they both lived and rode together. When we sat down, the first thing I said to both her and her mother who accompanied her, was since her grief was so raw and new, it might not matter what earth-shattering validation is brought forward by her husband - she wasn't likely to leave our session feeling any better. I even went as far as to say I typically wouldn't sit with someone so soon after a passing for that very reason, but when spirit sent a message to me through my daughter during our car ride, I simply couldn't ignore it. So I let her know that spirit arranged our meeting for a reason, and whatever that reason was, I trusted it was supposed to happen.

During our hour together, which was the first of many since then, her amazing husband spoke about compellingly accurate aspects of his and their lives, his passing, their families, and the list goes on. He spoke about his sudden and unexpected passing that happened outdoors, he talked about his life being a dream-come-true getting to do what he loved, he talked about his dogs, his dark-colored male horse who was still living, and about his large watch his wife had as well as his wedding ring. He spoke about validation after validation, and as I had expected, despite all the amazing things he proved that day, I felt at the time that she was hardly moved. And this was due to the fact that she simply missed him so badly. But if that same reading had taken place perhaps six months or a year later, that factual or validating information might have carried far more weight than I thought it did that day.

Because healing is a process, sitting with a Medium to experience proof of life after physical death is most powerful when we're truly ready to accept this as reality, and when we're additionally prepared to continue living our lives without our loved ones here with us. Generally speaking, this is not the case for most people so soon after losing someone.

As a testament to the healing process, however, many months, readings, and experiences later, both the young woman and her mother have grown and healed in incredible ways. There are still many parts yet to unfold on their journeys of healing and grief, but they have also now had many direct experiences with their loved ones, without the help of a Medium. And to a large extent, the sum total of all their experiences with Mediums, traditional learning through books, the passage of time, and the ever-present support and love from spirit has enabled them to *know* their loved ones walk with them, still. Their spirit loved ones are present in their lives, and they experience proof of that often.

Over time I came to learn there were many commonalities between me, my client, and her husband in spirit, with the most obvious connection being horses (I ride, as well). Second to that was they lived and trained near me some time before, though I had no knowledge of who either of them were. And finally, the day her husband passed was my birthday. I know for certain that spirit arranged our meeting, and I am eternally grateful for the experience. You are likely to find some synchronistic connections between yourself and some of your clients, as well.

Some Mediums have a minimum length of time for someone to be passed before they'll attempt to channel them, so as to allow spirit enough time to be able to 'come through'. But I don't subscribe to that idea, because spirit has proven time and again that, just as we're individuals, so are they. And some are ready and available to connect very shortly after their phys-ical passing, and others can take longer. With spirit, there's never a hard and fast rule - absolutely anything is possible.

The thing about being a Medium is that, as much as some people might really want to do the job, it's a really big one - with a lot of responsibility. You have to be prepared to deliver messages and information from the spirit world that may or may not be received well - for a number for reasons.

For example, I've channeled many loved ones who left the physical world by way of suicide. Many of those who I've sat with are parents, spouses, siblings, and they're often hoping to hear from spirit an answer to the big question of "why?".

Sometimes they aren't even sure whether or not what happened to their loved one was actually sui-cide, or an accident, and as a Medium, you have to be prepared to explore these questions with spirit. These aren't usually 'light conversations', and it takes a lot of skill to understand what spirit's saying, as some of the messages are very subtle but mark a clear dis-tinction between something like suicide or an uninten-tional or apathetic occurrence. And of course there is great responsibility in getting the message correct, as spirit (and your clients) are counting on you to repre-sent the spirit world, and the truth, itself.

These types of readings are often very emotional, and rightfully so. But as the medium between spirit and their loved ones here, it's so important to be as accu-rate as possible with what's being communicated, or you could end up causing emotional distress to your clients. Even the word suicide frequently carries with it stigma - an energy - that might be difficult for some to cope with. From that perspective, I encourage you to explore using different terminology for the sake of those who can't effectively manage a gut-response to the word in relation to their own loved one. This is by no means meant to scare you from working with clients who are dealing with something as emotional as losing a loved one to suicide. Just the opposite, in fact. I feel with more Mediums out there practicing, we will have more healing taking place on a global scale, and more importantly, the truth - that no matter how we leave this world, we all go to the same place - will be spread more widely. But I must also stress the importance of recognizing the immense impact your work can have on someone - so please, please, please, take your growth and development as a Medium seriously...and do your homework faithfully.

I recall a time when I had a family sitting with me for a reading - dad, mom, and daughter. Within seconds of sitting down, a young male stepped forward and snapped his fingers (my symbol that his passing was quick, sudden, or unexpected). He then transmitted to me the sensation of falling. But there was no fear - it was by choice. They understood immediately that their son and brother was with us at that exact moment. I was honored to bring this loving young man through for many reasons, with the most important being to help his parents and sister understand that he was well and perfect on the other side. His vibration, his state of being, his energy at the end of his physical life was so completely opposite of how he felt now, at home on the other side. His energy was joyful and loving. And it was so important for them to know their son and brother's soul existed in the same place as everyone else, and that he was happy. They were still struggling with the stigma associated with suicide, and they struggled even more with why it happened at all. I like to think I helped them in some way understand, through spirit, why this happens sometimes.

You see, spirit has confirmed to me that when something like suicide happens, it's usually because when we plan our lives during the pre-birth planning process, we estimate how much of our soul we need bring with us to make it through the lifetime. But because of free-will choices made along the way, sometimes our best laid plans aren't so easily achieved, and life is more difficult than we had planned. This is when it takes us more energy than we anticipated to continue through a lifetime. You can compare it to a bank account - we deposit a certain amount of funds (soul energy) into the account that are intended to support our lifetime here. But if we deplete that energy resource before our planned time of exit, how can we continue? Well spirit tells me the answer is that we can't. So we exit before our originally planned time. And while there are many soul lessons to be learned from these types of lifetimes, we still return to that most beautiful place. And that's what I wanted this young man's dad, mom, and sister to know that day. That their son and brother just couldn't continue, and on a soul level, he knew that he had to go.

In my career as a Medium, I've worked with families who lost their loved ones in a multitude of ways. Along with suicide, another way of passing that has proven to be exceptionally difficult for families to cope with is homicide. I once worked on a cold case where the bodies of the victims were never located. How I began working on the case was quite interesting, because I had no idea I was channeling the spirit of a missing person when I started the reading.

One spring afternoon, I met with a wonderful older gentleman for a reading and began bringing through a young male from the spirit world. Throughout the reading I felt something was different compared to a usual or typical reading. When the spirit boy talked about his passing, there was mystery there - something dubious. But he also spoke about beautiful and amazing memories, momentos, and facts about his life. He even vividly described a picture of himself and a new bike he wanted to acknowledge, to which is father (after the reading) responded by pulling out of his wallet a newspaper clipping with a picture of his son winning a brand-new bike. As I learned after the reading, that newspaper clipping had been kept in his wallet for over thirty years, and was his son's "Missing Person" advertisement in the local paper.

After the reading was over, we talked openly about what happened with his son, and this was when I learned that his son's disappearance was a cold case and a body was never found. So for this father, who never was given any physical proof that his son was no longer here in the physical world, I had just brought through significant evidence that the person I was channeling from the spirit world was his son. This particular experience, which was the first of many with this lovely older gentleman and the people close to him, was a significant reminder for me of the immense responsibility I have working as a Medium.

His son had disappeared with another boy nearly thirty years earlier. A few months after sitting with my client for the first time, my friend and colleague Lynn and I visited the property on request, and led by spirit we traveled the route taken by the boys that mysterious night. Lynn worked with spirit and divining rods to reaffirm the directions we were walking in, and I worked solely with spirit. We spent nearly two hours navigating this rural property, and while we did so, Lynn and I were physically separated from one another. I was in front of the group, and Lynn was just behind. When spirit came forward with specific information, I would turn around to Lynn and we would often simultaneously say the same thing, which was proof that spirit was present and guiding us. Much of the information offered by the boys was in some way validated by others who were present to watch our investigation. The information that has remained a mystery for decades was effortlessly communicated to us by spirit that day. The boys showed us how they were separated from one another, how they were killed, and by whom. We shared this information with the family, who informed us that much of the information is what they had suspected for all these years. But still, there has never been any concrete, irrefutable evidence to prove it, and closure still eludes my client to this day. All of these experiences were significant reminders of the immense responsibility I have working as a Medium, and how we have to take special care of the hearts we're working for.

It might seem hard to believe that as a spiritual worker, it's possible to cause harm to someone who sits with you for a reading. It might be hard to believe because surely your intentions are in the right place, but certainly there is a fine line between delivering information from spirit exactly as they give it to you, and delivering information from spirit that, with your interpretation, leaves your client feeling disempowered or distraught.

I'll give you an example of a Medium leaving a client disempowered, confused, and feeling uneasy. Believe it or not, I was the client! A few years ago I visited a fairly prominent spiritualist community, and though I didn't *need* to sit with another Medium, I followed the concept of 'When in Rome...'. So I sat with a Medium, and right off the hop, I let her know that I was also a Medium. I assumed because she was a spiritual worker, I didn't need to protect myself and that I could trust her in some way because surely her heart was in the right place. Well, as soon as the reading started, it became clear to me that accuracy would not be this Medium's strong-suit. And instead of making her do the work to bring forward accurate and detailed information, I accepted vague descriptions of things because as a Medium myself, I knew what spirit was trying to say. But

I never should have done that - and you shouldn't either. A Medium has a job, so just let them do it!

The reading went on this way for some time, and when we got near the end she asked if there was someone else I had wanted to hear from. I said there wasn't, but mentioned someone connected to me who rarely comes through to other Medium colleagues when I'm working with them. Then, without providing validation she said she was connected to this person I had mentioned in spirit. She said my loved one who I don't hear from often didn't make it to the other side, and said they are stilling hanging around where they used to live. She said my loved one was disapproving of the spiritual work I was doing, and that in terms of soul-level progression, my loved one hadn't done any. My jaw. On the floor.

As the words were coming out of her mouth, not an ounce of it rang true for me. But still, where did she come up with that? I teeter-tottered between trusting my higher self, and doubting all of the work I had ever done up until that point. Could this Medium be correct? If so, how come I never picked up on it myself? I left the reading feeling upset at the experience. I meditated on it and shared the information with friends who traveled with me. We all meditated, and we all gave each other healing to overcome the energetic turmoil that was occurring in my gut and theirs.

As we left that place, I was acutely aware that this was a tremendous growth and learning opportunity for me. Just because someone works with the light (or claims to), it means nothing. A genuine, loving, spirit-guided experience has to occur authentically, and leaving yourself wide-open when working with someone who you don't know, even a spiritual practitioner, isn't a good idea. I think the best way to work with a Medium or spiritual healer is to begin with an open heart, but lead with your gut - your intuition. Don't accept things that don't ring true - that don't feel right, deep down in your soul. You aren't obligated to accept or believe everything someone says just because you chose to sit with them for a spiritual session. It's your right to decide what your truth is, and I encourage you to look to yourself to be the judge during the formation of your own personal truth. Not a guru, not an advanced practitioner, not a mentor - you. Just you. My experience with that Medium on that day again reminded me of the immense responsibility I have as a Medium.

In mediumship, I'll always encourage you to give what you get - meaning, if spirit shows you a room full of boxes, tell your client spirit's showing you a room full of boxes. If they can't understand it literally, you can move to symbology - are they moving, is someone significant moving, did their loved one work in real estate, etc. But if spirit shows you something that feels perhaps negative or non-supportive, or questionable in terms of what feels like light and love, you have consider being very careful about how you're going to articulate the message to your client. Beyond that, you also have to question your own perception and interpretation of what spirit's showing you, because their true nature is love, support, and light. If you feel something that strays from that true nature, then I simply suggest you sit with the information a little longer, ask spirit to elaborate or clarify, and run it by your spirit guide before you decide to share your interpretation with your client.

What you say to your clients has the power to enlighten and uplift them, and conversely, your words have the ability to disempower and hurt them. So do take precious care in how you speak the messages from the spirit world. Because after all, we're working with spirit to help provide the highest and best for all.

CHAPTER 12
Some Final Words From Spirit

You'll start to notice over time that there are common messages that spirit brings forward. These messages will also be key in what forms your own personal truths about certain spiritual things, because you'll see the messages repeated over and over from the spirit world. Through these messages you'll also come to genuinely know the true nature of spirit - which is love!

I always say there are two reasons why spirit connects with us during mediumship. The first is because they want you to know they're okay - that they still exist, and that you will too, because we are all souls of consciousness that survive physical death. And the second reason is to help you heal through messages.

Those of us here in the physical world who have lost someone often wonder if they're okay - are they safe, do they miss us, are they healthy now? I can tell you from my experience, the answer to those questions is always yes. What I know from spirit is that when we pass and shed our physical bodies, we're greeted by our loved ones who transitioned to spirit before us, as well as our angels and guides. During that period of transition to spirit (which, by the way, can occur before our actual last physical breath here on earth), there is no fear and there is no hurt. There is warmth, comfort, ease, bliss.

While I know this to be true from spirit, I encourage you to do some research on the topic of Near-Death Experiences. You're sure to find some extremely compelling evidence that supports the belief of an afterlife. Many accounts will be exceptionally similar to one another - accounts of total and complete strangers seemingly experiencing consciousness after physical death. Near-Death Experiences is a fascinating topic and many, many hours can be spent researching it.

What else does spirit often say in their messages through Mediums? I could probably write several chapters on just that topic! But here I'll share with you just some of the most common messages from heaven.

1. Their passing couldn't be prevented. So many loved ones left behind struggle with the question of whether or not they could have done something differently, and death been prevented. Spirit's answer is always the same. It's "no". In mediumship readings where this question is mentioned, spirit will usually ask me to explain the idea or concept of pre-birth planning. For the purposes of understanding this common message from spirit, I'll provide a very elementary and brief overview of what pre-birth planning is, and I encourage you to learn and understand this concept at greater lengths as part of your evolving practice.

Pre-birth planning is a spiritual concept and reality and that we plan the major lessons and happenings in our life, including when we pass (which can be a choice of several options commonly referred to as 'exit points'). We devise our pre-birth plan while we're on the other side, before we incarnate into this lifetime. The lessons we plan are chosen by us because on a soul level, they're what we need to experience in order to progress. And all of those lessons and experiences we plan for ourselves are agreed to by all others in our soul group. This part of the theory of pre-birth planning can be a hard pill for people to swallow after losing someone close to them, because it implies they agreed, as part of their sacred contract between themselves and their loved one, that they would lose them in the way and at the time they did. So many people have said, "I can't believe that I agreed to lose to my child," or "I can't believe that I agreed to watch my loved one suffer so much". I understand those sentiments, but for me, I can't argue a point that has been communicated so endlessly and without waiver or variation from heaven.

The concept of pre-birth planning suggests that we can not change the major lessons to be learned that we originally planned for ourselves. But we still have free-will choice that can determine if and how exactly we end up learning our chosen lessons. We can choose how we respond to things that happen to us. We can choose to grow, heal, expand. Alternatively, we can choose to not recover, not embrace love, not grow. These free-will choices can determine how we get to accomplishing our life lessons, and in fact can determine whether not we get there at all.

If we don't learn, heal, and grow from our pre-planned lessons during this lifetime, we are sure to live similar experiences in subsequent lifetimes until we've mastered those lessons. For example, imagine a person whose heart was broken by the indiscretions of a spouse, and for years and years, against the encouragement of people around them to heal, they held on tightly to the anger, to the betrayal. Their normal state of being became a very low vibration, and life no longer inspired them. Even until their last day on earth, they couldn't let the light of happiness and love into their life. Spirit says that somewhere between when they learned about the indiscretion and the time they passed, they had a choice about how they would respond to the hurdle. They could respond as they did, and not heal, not grow from it, not survive it. Or they could have done a lot more. They could have chosen to heal - and this is what our soul intends to happen, but it doesn't always work out that way. And so when we choose to not learn our planned lessons, we end up repeating them, energetically speaking - either in this lifetime by recycling through the same negative patterns, or into the next lifetime where we might expect to have the same things happen to us so as to create the learning opportunity for our soul to heal once again.

2. They are happy, and they want you to be, too. Spirit never carries with them anger, resentment, disapproval, or discord. They know only love. In readings, people will often say something like, "I don't know why they're mentioning my Aunt Marie - they never got along." But that's exactly why they're mentioning her - because they want you to know they're sending love, and that in heaven there is no judgment, and conflict doesn't make the transition to spirit, because the low energy of conflict, anger, and hate simply can't be sustained in such an overwhelmingly high vibration.

Another question that sometimes comes up during readings is whether or not a spirit loved one is okay with their partner dating or meeting someone new. And again, the answer is always yes (unless there's something specific about the new person in their spouse's life that they aren't exactly keen on). Loved ones on the other side always want your happiness, and that almost always means moving on with your life, at the pace that's right for each individual. They want us to find love again - in whatever shape or form that may be in.

Spirit also lets me know that they don't 'miss' us the way we miss them. It's different. They're so deeply connected with us from the other side. In many ways, they're more deeply connected to us now than they were when they were here. Sadness is an emotion that plainly doesn't exist on the other side. Love is all encompassing, and our time apart from our spirit loved ones moves much faster on the other side, where time and space are not linear as we perceive them here. As I know it from spirit, our time physically apart from them, from their perspective, is faster than the blink of an eye.

3. They're with you often, and they try to let you know that. Spirit's with us often - when we need or want them to be, or when they want to be here. What I know from spirit is they give us signs they're around us. When we're able to acknowledge those signs coming from them, (e.g., we say, "Thank you, Dad - I know you're here,") they become elated. They feel tremendous joy when we know they're here.

There are some common signs from spirit, that once pointed out, are easy to recognize. They include thinking about your loved one randomly and seemingly out of nowhere (this means they're near you). You could have the telephone ring and when you pick it up, no one's there, or a butterfly or bird might catch your eye or come unusually close to you. A dime or penny might be found in an unanticipated place, or children may make reference to a loved one they never met or can't remember. Or you could see or hear a loved one's name somewhere unexpected. Glancing at the clock as it strikes 11:11, 1:11, 3:33, or another repetitive number is another sure sign that spirit's near you. Spirit may also give a sign that's very unique to them. For example, a sign from my Dad when he's near is the Eiffel Tower, which relates to something special to me. You see, my last name before I married was Latour, which is a French surname. The Eiffel Tower in French is spelled la Tour Eiffel. So when I see the Eiffel Tower, I also see my Dad's last name - Latour! Spirit can also transmit the perception of a scent to us - like a perfume, after-shave, or even cigarette or cigar smoke.

Soon after having my son, I was laying in bed with him one morning when my mother-in-law in spirit stepped forward. We spoke for a long time about my son, her first grandson. I asked her for a sign or symbol for people to recognize when she's near. Surprisingly, she showed me a spiral. I asked her why she chose that symbol, but she didn't answer me - she just smiled. Within a week, the spiral symbol began flooding our lives - mine, my husband's, and our children's. It was amazing.

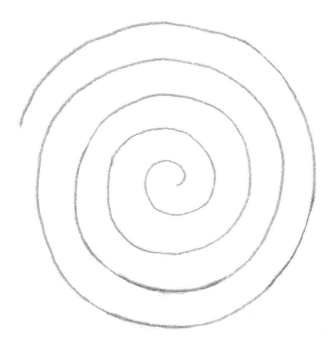

The first sign came from my daughter who drew it on the shower door and said, "Look mummy, it's a dizzy". I asked her where she learned that symbol, and not surprisingly, she said she didn't know. About a week later I was visiting my horse, and as I walked past his stall door, my heart leaped. Drawn in chalk on Ralphie's stall was a spiral. I laughed and exclaimed to myself, "No way!" Next was a couple of weeks after that, and we were at a family reunion at a conservation area. A few hours into the reunion I had to head out, but Ryan stayed with August and Culzean. About an hour after leaving, Ryan sent me a picture of a piece of confetti he found under the chair I was sitting in. Guess what shape it was? You got it - a spiral! This is a small handful of the spiral sign my mother-in-law has given us and continues to give. It's always wonderful seeing her signs all around us.

I encourage you to share with others these common signs and symbols from spirit. There are so many people who have no idea that they're supported by the spirit world, and it may just brighten their day, or their life, to learn or experience the signs for themselves.

4. They want you to embrace forgiveness. Forgiveness is more about you than the person you're forgiving. Practicing forgiveness releases us from the grip of anger and resentment. In fact, we can forgive someone without ever telling them we do, because forgiveness isn't necessarily about giving to someone else - it's about giving ourselves the relief that comes from no longer suffering the anger, resentment, and pain.

I remember a reading with a client where their mother stepped forward, and within minutes she was talking about the name of woman whom my client detested. She shuddered at the name coming out of my mouth. As soon as I felt her energetic reaction, I knew that spirit was bringing it up because they were encouraging forgiveness. You see, my client held that woman accountable for her father's death. She held on so tightly to that anger and sadness, and her mother was asking her to consider releasing those emotions for her greater good.

As I learned later, my client had recently experienced a dream visitation from that woman whose mere name repulsed here (that woman was now in spirit). She couldn't figure out why she was visiting her, but understood now, after communicating with her mom on the other side, that her team of spirit helpers was asking her to embrace forgiveness. That tightness in her chest was getting heavier, and heavier, and from spirit's all knowing and loving perspective on the other side, they were giving her insight that now was the time to heal.

Take notice that when I talk about messages or guidance from spirit, I use words like 'consider' or 'encourage' rather than 'tell'. Spirit rarely gives directives, because they can't make decisions for you. And they won't. But they can give you some of their insight and perspective, which is always enlightening and helpful.

A great mentor, friend, and colleague of mine is Lynn, who I have mentioned a few times in this book. Lynn has spent most of her life working in justice - in restorative justice, particularly. Restorative justice is a type of criminal justice that focuses on the rehabilitation of offenders through reconciliation with victims and the community. Lynn spent many years pioneering restorative justice programs, and she's also an incredibly talented Medium, healer, psychic, shamanic practitioner, and conventional teacher. Teaching forgiveness is a major part of her life's work, and since the message of embracing forgiveness is given from the spirit world so often, I was honored when Lynn agreed to share her wisdom on the topic with you for this book.

The Journey of Forgiveness
By: Lynn Zammit

Forgiveness is a journey that each soul takes as it strives for perfection or enlightenment. When we have been harmed in some way our first reaction is often one of grief, fear, anger, resentment or revenge. If we do not find healthy ways to release these negative emotions they become part of who we are, both energetically and emotionally and this "dis-ease" in the body often manifests as illness eventually. For some, these negative emotions come to define who and what we are. We can see ourselves as a 'victim' and as such, peer out at the world through a victim lens defining who we are by what has happened to us. Medical research shows that those who can't forgive the harms done to them tend to have negative indicators of health and wellbeing including more stress- related disorders, lower immune system function, higher rates of cardiovascular disease as well as higher rates of divorce. For victims of even the most heinous crimes, finding the strength to forgive can be incredibly healing and life-affirming. It offers them a way back into the light.

Forgiveness is also a powerful antidote for those who cause harm. There is much healing to be found when those who have caused harm can be forgiven. When we acknowledge that this person who harmed us is more than just those bad deeds, when we can see them as also being a person who got lost along the way or perhaps were also a victim at some point in their life, we can help them move forward as well. Those who have caused harm often feel unworthy of our forgiveness and that self-forgiveness is a very important part of their soul journey, to see themselves as worthy of forgiveness and love.

In the countless studies on the power of forgiveness the research clearly shows that ultimately forgiveness is not something we do for the other person but something we do for ourselves. It is a letting go of the power that the harm has over you. It is releasing all the negative emotions associated with the harm so that you can set that burden down. It is not excusing the harmful behavior, or pretending that it did not happen, but it is allowing the soul to move beyond the pain, to pick up the broken pieces and get on with the job of living the life you were meant to live. Forgiveness allows us to write our own ending to that painful chapter. It is releasing the hope that things could have been different.

On a spiritual level, if we can begin to see the greater soul plan for our lives then we can acknowledge that those who have harmed us have also made it possible for us to learn some of our most important soul lessons. This awareness of the amazing power of forgiveness is often expressed during a Past Life Regression when the client's past life soul has left the body and is journeying to the other side. It is at this point that we do a life review and most times they will express a profound understanding of why other people acted the way they did. At that higher soul level we begin to realize that most people do the best they can do under the circumstances, with the knowledge, skills and understanding they possess. When we know better we do better. As the soul passes over this flood of forgiveness fills them as they see each person for the divine being that they are. Sometimes, during Shamanic healing work we have to trace back through an ancestral line and offer forgiveness and healing to past generations in order to clear up energies that are passed down through families.

It is not by accident that thirteen of the world's major religions all share the same teaching which, in the Christian version, asks us to "do unto others as you would have them do unto you". In our many lives we have all been saints and sinners, beggars and kings. It would serve us well to remember that forgiveness is a door that swings both ways. When our loved ones on the other side come with messages of forgiveness it is because they understand the power that it holds...on both sides of the veil.

My hope is that as you've read through this book, you've expanded in some way to allow spirit in. You have a whole team of helpers on the other side - your angels, guides, loved ones, and divine source, who all want to help you. As we evolve and come to know the spirit world, healing happens and everything around us changes. If you've read this book, then you're likely among those who are guided to bridge the gap between this world and the next. I'm honored to have helped you on that important journey, and I wish you the highest love and light! Take that light, that truth, and pass it out to the world.

Made in the USA
Middletown, DE
20 October 2023

41155526R00080